THE CHANCE TO LIVE MORE
THAN ONCE

THE CHANCE TO LIVE MORE THAN ONCE

...Developing Future Lives and Careers

Barry Curnow
John McLean Fox

2000

First published in Great Britain in 1997 by Management Books 2000 Ltd,
Cowcombe House,
Cowcombe Hill,
Chalford,
Gloucestershire GL6 8HP
Tel: 01285-760722. Fax: 01285-760708

Printed and bound in Great Britain by The Orbital Press, Letchworth

British Library Cataloguing in Publication Data is available

ISBN 1-85252-286-0

Foreword

'Tempora mutantur, et nos mutamur in illis' – times change and we change with them. So wrote Harrison in his *Description of Britain* – in 1577. As it was then, so it is now, four hundred years later; we have to change as the times, like it or not.

I was in my late forties when I realised that I was going to have to change if I was to fit the times ahead. I was, it seemed, running out of jobs. I had got as far as I was going to get in my chosen profession. Even if I wanted to mark time for fifteen more years in my present role, it was extremely unlikely that I would be allowed to do so. Younger people were both cheaper and more up-to-date, and huffing and puffing about age discrimination was not going to change that basic fact. I concluded that I would have to rethink my assumptions about my career, my way of life and, crucially, my finances if I wanted life to go on being an interesting and rewarding experience.

I did not know it then, but I was planning for my Third Age, for that period of life beyond the career job and parenting which can last for anything up to thirty years. It was not going to be retirement – I had no wish to be idle for that long and certainly could not afford to be. There had to be work, but it clearly was not going to be the sort of full-time work I had been accustomed to. I was going to have to be much more self-sufficient. There would be no one drawing up career plans for me, arranging training courses or even booking tickets. More worrying than that, however, was my discovery that I would have to sit down and think what sort of life I wanted. I had become conditioned to weekday jobs, annual pay rises and annual holidays. Success had meant more seniority and more money. I had been compiling a curriculum vitae but, suddenly, there was no one interested in looking at it. What was life about, I asked myself, when a C.V. no longer mattered?

I felt that I was looking out onto a wide uncharted sea, one on which I would, in honesty, have preferred not to venture. I cannot pretend that the voyage I then embarked on was all easy going but it has been interesting. In retrospect, more than ten years on, I would not have had it otherwise. I now know that the Third Age is not a euphemism for old age or even for retirement. It is a new way of life, one with more choices and more problems, a chance to do and be something different, but also a challenge to cope with. I now know, too, that it is a stage in life which will happen to almost everyone of us, because if we reach fifty in reasonable health we are unlikely to die before we are in our late seventies yet will increasingly be leaving our career jobs in our fifties. That gap is the Third Age and before too long nearly one third of all adults will be in it.

Some changes are cyclical, they reverse themselves. This one will not. Organisations will need fewer and shorter career posts as they strip themselves down for a more technological age. At the same time, most of us are, I trust, going to live even more healthily for longer. The gap between the end of the job and the start of senility gets bigger. We shall have to change our picture of life's normal course to fit these changing times and stop deluding ourselves that it will not happen to us. When we take that on board we will realise that it is only common-sense to prepare for this Third Age more seriously and more realistically. That is true for the individual but it is also true for the organisation. The sensible organisation will want to find a way to continue to draw on the experience and skills of its people even when it cannot afford to keep them on the full-time payroll. The decent organisation will want to help its people make the best use of this unexpected gift of time.

This book, therefore, is made for our times. It is badly needed. I hope that it will be priority reading for every working person approaching mid-life, particularly those employed as executives or professional people in different fields. The issues it discusses are the stuff of personal survival and fulfilment. To drift into the Third Age is a sure way of discovering the problems without the opportunities. I wish only that it had been available to me when I first set out on that uncharted sea a decade or more ago. Nor could I have wished for better pilots that the two authors of this book. They bring with them long experience of the subject, an active involvement in counselling both individuals and organisations and much insight into what is needed. We have much to learn both from them and from the methodology which they describe.

Charles Handy
March 1997

Contents

1

Introduction

The Chance To Live More Than Once will mark the start of an important journey for those readers moving into their Third Age, that rich time between ending your main career and deciding to rest and recline! You will make choices, follow leads, change your mind, then try something else until you strike the right balance of career, domesticity and personal ambition in this fruitful third phase of your life. For those well into the Third Age you will be able to reflect upon where you are now and how to enhance the value and satisfaction of what you do. For those who are still in the Second Age of the main career phase, this book will provide food for thought on what the future of work holds for you as well as ideas and tools for planning to use the opportunities open to you. Times are changing and the context of this book is one of shifting work patterns, portfolio careers and post employment status. This is a practical, self-help handbook for all ages, especially those within sight of their Third Age.

However, this is a self-help book with a difference. It does not offer the promise of something for nothing like *The Lazy Man's Way to Riches* by Joe Karbo or even a quicker route to the secrets of success like the deservedly acclaimed *The Seven Habits of Highly Effective People* by Stephen Covey. It has certain things in common with both of these best-sellers in that it deals with some universal human principles and helps to share others' experience of navigating potentially treacherous pathways, as a way of learning from them.

Nor is *The Chance to Live More Than Once* like the legendary

Making Friends and Influencing People by Dale Carnegie, *The Power of Positive Thinking* by Norman Vincent Peal or the latter-day *Unlimited Power* and *Awaken the Giant Within* by Anthony Robbins, who on his trips to Britain had hundreds of managers patiently lining up in a car park to literally walk on hot coals, which the overwhelming majority of them did without flinching! These books all help to elicit personal resourcefulness as a means of becoming more effective with others to be happier and more fulfilled in one's relationships both in and out of work, but none of them deals with the new realities of life after careers and work after employment.

The Chance to Live More Than Once is more of a guerrilla warfare handbook, a do-it-yourself survival kit for life after the main career, a guide to personal resourcefulness and to sustaining a livelihood in the world beyond employment, where all of us now have to test our employability and market effectiveness.

Nearly thirty years ago, it was clear to one of the authors that the planning and development tools used by major corporations for growing their businesses and their people were too important to be restricted to organisations, because individuals needed them for running their own lives. In those days of the late sixties most people assumed that it was the responsibility of employers to manage the careers opportunities and in effect the very lives of their employees. Counselling was for the sick, the troubled and weak, while planning was for accountants and economists. The legacy of *truth, love and flower power* carried over from the sixties made the concept of Total Life Counselling Ltd, a company which we started then but never traded, far too advanced for its time. When Michael Heseltine spoke at the launch of Future Perfect (Counselling) Ltd in 1989, the company that carried out the researches and programmes on which this book is based, the idea seemed to have come of age and he introduced the new company with the words 'past tense, Future Perfect'.

Well, the future is here and it feels increasingly tense as we approach the millennium. Individual citizens are now fighting a civil war in the midst of a revolution where it's not at all clear who is the legitimate authority and who is overthrowing whom. The cause is survival, the battleground is the markets where we maintain our employability and the battlefront is the means of earning our livelihoods and supporting our resourcefulness and humanity in the communities where we work, and hopefully continue to grow our capacities and fulfil our potentials.

The twin imperatives of physical and financial survival and personal and psychological growth call for both resourcefulness and life-planning. This should go hand in hand with the support of what Charles Hampden-Turner has called *the helping stranger*, a consultant, coach, teacher, counsellor or 'friend' who is detached but committed to your cause and well-being. Maybe this book will turn out to be a *helping stranger* in your life-planning?

The life-planning required is not necessarily planning in a deterministic, mechanical, achievement-seeking way, although the disciplines of such a systematic approach work well and reassuringly for some people. This approach to life-planning is more in the spirit of the definition of careers provided by the late Professor Alec Rodger, former Professor of Occupational Psychology at Birkbeck College in the University of London. He said that 'careers consist of a series of planned procrastinations'. He did not mean this in a *laissez-faire* sense and he was certainly not advocating abdication! He was proposing that keeping one's options open and the range of choices maximised, together with maintaining a weather eye for opportunities and how to seize them, was actually a very sensible strategy for career and life progression in changing and uncertain employment markets. This observation is even more true today.

When Future Perfect started all those of us involved in its creation were still in our main careers (for the story of Future Perfect, see Appendix 1). Now we are in our second careers and in a sense our second lives. So the Future Perfect story is the story of our own experience as we have lived through the Third Age life transition as well as the stories of thousands of our clients and course participants over the years.

William James, the 19th-century psychologist, divided people into what he called *once born* and *twice born*. The once born were conformists who joined in and took their identity from the communities, societies and times in which they lived, often very passionately and energetically, but *they went with the flow*. The *twice born* according to James were more detached from others, had a sense of themselves as apart and often appeared somewhat rootless, thrusting, restless, so were *with but not of the crowd*. The first group were joiners and the second group leaders.

Career and hence life success for those employed within organisations in recent times has required *once born* rather than *twice born* behaviour in order to climb the corporate ladder. (So much so that several observers have noted that the career behaviour required to rise to the top of the corporate ladder in our major organisations has typically been diametrically opposite to the leadership skills that need to be exercised on arrival at the top – refer to Alistair Mant in *The Rise and Fall of the British Manager*.) Now, it seems that increasingly everybody needs to be twice born. We need to have the resourcefulness and self-reliance to equip ourselves for economic survival and also to prepare ourselves psychologically *to be and to become the person we were born to be*.

In one sense this book is about deep psychological and spiritual matters but we have tried to adopt a non-technical, non-religious and pragmatic approach. Certainly no specialist knowledge beyond life experience and a capacity to learn from self and others is required. It is a practical handbook for making meaning in the Third Age of our lives, in the search for human effectiveness, which we interpret as fulfilment, as well as holding on where appropriate to the efficiency emphasised in the First and Second Ages of our lives when pursuing our main careers.

The authors are both management consultants with more than 50 years of experience between them. This means that we have spent our main careers helping people to improve their organisational efficiency and personal effectiveness in corporate careers and markets. In the last seven years we have been working through Future Perfect to apply those principles to helping people become resourceful and effective in seeking and securing productive endeavour after their main careers.

When we had reached senior positions in our respective organisations, John as a Director of PA Management Consultants and Barry as Chairman and Chief Executive of Hay-MSL, both leading human resource management consultancy groups, we were deeply involved in issues concerning the second half of life, with the management and motivation of mature employees in organisations and increasingly with helping people as they left organisations at younger and younger ages. As Chairman of MSL Barry was involved in the too-old-at-40 campaign to discourage age discrimination in management and professional appointments, a campaign which continued during his period as President of the then Institute of Personnel Management, when major research on age policy was commissioned and the IPM Statement on Age and Employment was issued (Appendix 2).

But avoiding discrimination in employment is only one part of the story which applies to a shrinking employed workforce. The other side of the equation is personal preparation for life after the main career and planning for employability and gainful endeavour in the Third Age, that period which is a gift from medical science which has extended our healthy life expectancy by at least twenty-five years during this century alone. So many people have said to us, 'If only I had started planning earlier'. It is this life-planning with which Future Perfect has been principally engaged, helping individuals and organisations deal with inevitable personal and corporate change.

A couple of years ago we wrote a book about our work with corporations to help them not only to avoid discrimination in employing older people but also to adopt policies that help to maximise potential for the experienced resource of the mature workforce. Then as now we were influenced profoundly by the young people with whom we work as well as our more mature personal and business friends. The principles and requirements with which we are concerned in this present volume apply equally to all age groups, although we are conscious that for our younger colleagues our assumptions about corporate life and individual endeavour may be less fashionable or self-evident, needing explanation and rationale or even interpretation and justification. But our work with all ages convinces us that we are dealing with some enduring human imperatives here as well as with the spirit of the times. The corporate cultures in which we explored the adventures and fought the career campaigns of our own Second Age warrior years may be obsolescent species of organisation, if not dinosaurs, but we see exactly comparable patterns of behaviour and requirements in the post-employment markets and the networked communities and co-operative assemblies and communities that are replacing them.

Our theme is the same as in that earlier book but here we talk of our work with individuals rather than corporations and we have been influenced by a new text: *The Empty Raincoat* by Charles Handy (Hutchinson, London). Charles Handy was an early and remains a continuing inspiration of Future Perfect.

We need look no further for clues to equipping our organisations to see beyond tomorrow, the implications of the changing workforce. Twelve years ago Barry became Group Managing Director of Hay-MSL. In that year of 1984, Charles Handy addressed the Hay Group Annual Client meeting and made some predictions about changes in the workforce. Four years later at the Hay European Client meeting in Rome, his tomorrow of the Shamrock organisation had become reality today and now it's almost part of our yesterdays. The Shamrock organisation has arrived and three years ago when he spoke to a Maresfield Curnow School of Management Consulting Brainstrust Workshop Seminar, he predicted that the federal organisation was the organisational form of the future. It's here today. Tom Peters, when he was in London and on British television last autumn, was referring to Charles Handy's thinking as the thing of today. So having established Charles' credentials as one of the few European management gurus, we should note that he now predicts that by the year 2000, half as many people will be paid twice as much for working three times as hard.

We have been very fortunate in our careers, not only to work with clients on these radical changes but also to be some kind of experimental guinea pigs, in also ourselves living through the work force changes that he has predicted and their consequences for our own families and in our lives and careers. In this book we want to share some thoughts with you based on that experience. In the context of the changing workforce, these two areas of occupational endeavour – personnel management and management consulting – have been undergoing a classical structural change of industrial consolidation and melt-down, with changing boundaries, shifting segments and the different players 'paddling in each other's swimming pools': the personnel manager is becoming more like a management consultant, the management consultant is becoming more like a temporary executive or counsellor and the chief executive, in order to survive, is having to become much more of a crystal ball gazer and professor of the future, like Charles Handy. In fact we all need to be our own crystal ball gazers.

It's very confusing but also very exciting for those committed to personal growth and development and for whom continuous learning is a way of working and living rather than an empty slogan or even an 'Empty Raincoat'. Our theme, which continues from our previous book, is that individuals themselves are not immune from the strategic shifts taking place for organisations but are subject to the same changing macro-economic, geo-political and social forces that are impacting organisations and economies.

On the one hand employers who fail to acknowledge that work forces have radically changing lives and shapes of their own have a high risk of failure in adapting their organisations to their market and competitive environments because we live in revolutionary times. We make no apology for using that 'r' word because the essence of a revolution is that of irreversible change, that things will never be the same again, and vis-a-vis the workforce those organisations who wish to equip themselves to look beyond tomorrow must accept the revolutionary logic of irreversible change, of things never, ever being the same again.

On the other hand individuals must revolutionise their thinking in order to survive. So, What's the Big Idea Now?

The Big Idea

It was that *security comes from the outside*, that the success of a career comes from the employer. Our economic survival was *dependent* on an employer as provider.

We assumed the ideal of a *single, monolithic career*, no matter how many times reality and experience belied that concept. We accepted that rewards were about *having in the future,* and deferring our gratifications now for material gain and psychic recognition later.

The Big Idea was that we achieved and expressed our motivation through doing, acting, and visible achievement in the external career world. Now there is a new Big Idea and it is very different.

The New Big Idea

It is that *security comes from the inside*, from the work itself, from within relationships, through independence and above all through *marketability*. One needs the ability to sell one's self, through the versatility to spot, seize and adapt to many careers. Careers will be increasingly developed and pursued in parallel through living what we have called the *portfolio life*.

With the new Big Idea, *satisfaction is in being now*, not *having tomorrow*.

The Problem

The problem is that these two big ideas are so very different. People brought up on the first idea can be caught unawares and are liable to experience great culture shock when they come face to face with the reality of having to live according to the new big idea. However, the two ideas can be reconciled if the change is abrupt and comes without warning or the opportunity to plan.

Crisis: Breakdown or Breakthrough?

This can and frequently does lead to *human crisis*. This is a crisis of the spiritual kind, not in the religious sense but in the psychological sense, of *loss of purpose and meaning*. The discontinuity experienced by many may be likened for practical purposes to an unexpected bereavement of a close friend or relative: this is because of the loss of supports, boundaries, reference points, and in many cases the loss of identity or, as Alvin Toffler once put it, 'everything that was nailed down is coming loose'. Such loss – of identity, hope, benchmarks, sense of safety and security – is profoundly disorientating, and may be likened in turn to the aftermath of war, tragedy or disaster.

The problem is accentuated and can be more frightening because *we don't know what we don't know in a know-how society!* The rate of change in knowledge is exponential and yet it is only knowing what to expect to some degree that can reduce the phenomenal shock and stress of translating the once born chrysalis of employment into the born again butterfly of the post-employment society which can make the chance to live for a second time exciting and challenging.

Transformation Is Needed

Clearly, something much more fundamental than transition from work to retirement or from the principal life stage of the main career to the Third Age is involved in this transformation process. One must achieve sustainable resources and relationships in the new worlds of markets.

Yet, true paradigm shifts are emotionally and intellectually wrenching. The past often gets mislocated in the future and prevents our living to the full in the here and now of today.

The context for our book is: *'The Future of Work is not what it used to be'* and in the following chapters we aim to provide a map to navigate the pathways to *'The Chance To Live More Than Once'*.

2

The Impact Of Corporate Change On Individual Employees

An article in the *Independent* in 1995 by Howard Davies, when Director General of the CBI, based on Anthony Sampson's book *Company Man: The Rise and Fall of Corporate Life,* is entitled 'Company Man Takes a Dive'. It is a very expressive description of what many of us have experienced over the last decade or so. Womb to tomb employment is out and long-term employability is in. But do corporate bodies recognise this? And if so, what are they doing to help employees achieve it? There is still a long way to go in our view. In another article on the same topic in *People Management*, entitled 'Don't Downsize the Soul of the Organisation Too', Howard Davies refers to the inevitability of the staffing reductions caused by delayering, downsizing and re-engineering, but cautions organisations about the implications on a firm's people. 'The soul of the organisation lives in those people who have committed their lives, or a good part of those lives, to it....and this soul is also an important contributor to the bottom line. So a renewed contract with these people is a key element in any re-engineering process.' He then goes on to suggest that companies should be seeking to offer long-term 'employability' to overcome such difficulties.

Gareth Rees, Chief Executive of the change management consultants Kinsley Lord, highlights the pitfalls of business process re-engineering in an article that appeared in *Focus in Change Management* journal, February 1994. He puts forward an imaginary legal case against the process, and the lawyer for the plaintiffs (the people employed by the firm) addresses the jury initially as follows:

> 'Ladies and gentlemen of the jury, you are here to consider a most serious case – that a juggernaut called Re-engineering has inflicted psychological and social harm on my clients, the employees of Cosyfirm Ltd. Our case is not that Re-engineering is intrinsically bad. Indeed, my clients had hoped that in addition to improving efficiency, it would improve the quality of their working lives. Our case is that the company has been negligent in the way in which it has applied Re-engineering, and as a result has failed to achieve some of its objectives and has increased the stress and reduced the quality of the lives of its employees. Re-engineering was introduced eighteen months ago and is now largely complete. As our witnesses will acknowledge, it has produced real benefits for Cosyfirm and its customers. But they will also testify to the unnecessary pain and stress it has caused them as people, the damage to their self-esteem and the opportunities lost to the firm, because their skills and knowledge have not been tapped to the full.'

He then illustrates the weaknesses of poor Re-engineering implementation through putting the Head of Engineering, a Sales Representative, a Team Leader, a Fitter and a Product Development Process Owner in the witness box, and each story makes some telling points about the gaps that can open up during the change process.

Amin Rajan, Director of the Centre of Research in Employment and Technology in Europe (CREATE), recently explored personnel and employment issues in 'the City' for the London Human Resource Group; the findings appear in their report 'Winning People' (1994). He also warns against the trends in organisations of neglecting the motivational factors in the pursuit of performance-driven, jobless growth. He comments that there is no guarantee that business process re-engineering projects will produce the required level of anticipated benefits, and claims that the main motivators in this bleak climate are twofold – fear of redundancy and greed for money. Consequently these are the tools that have been used by many firms to achieve a culture change programme, communicated implicitly by fear through changed systems. Fear, he claims, leads in practice to risk aversion, an increase in bureaucracy, people looking where to jump next rather than performing well, and consequently a destructively high turnover rate in the City (25 per cent at the time; should be only 6 to 7 per cent in his view). He suggests that such an approach needs standing on its head and that, in order to take real advantage of the high productivity potential available, it is necessary to create a *winning culture* that will harness the motivation and commitment of the people involved. The report offers the conclusion that success depends on leadership and wanting to win.

We would certainly concur with this view, and would draw particular attention to the impact that organisational change has on both those who might ultimately leave and those who survive. If this ongoing level of change is to be addressed satisfactorily, a broader and much more imaginative view should surely be taken by the organisation of an employee's life and career development than is currently the case. The majority of organisations, however, with notable exceptions, appear to concentrate on training or self-development in conventional business areas rather than on personal, diversified development activities – and you can see why, because there is little likelihood of any immediate pay-off. In future, though, we believe that the employability aspect will receive a great deal more attention and that the capability of firms to promote this feature will achieve a much higher profile both internally and externally. We would even go so far as to say that the quality of an 'employability development' programme might well be a determining factor in attracting high-calibre recruits in the years to come. Most employees are looking for a tangible replacement to job security, which barely seems to exist in current and forecast scenarios. So if an organisation were able to promise that it would help you to develop new skills that would be beneficial to a future career outside the company, wouldn't that be irresistibly attractive?

Ford's imaginative Employee Development and Assistance Programme (described in our previous book) goes some way towards this and encourages employees to learn new leisure or career skills;

the company will fund courses up to a given level each year, and the offer is open to all employees. Some firms promote personal employee interests, such as Rolls Royce, who offer facilities for former employees to restore old aero engines, and Thomas Cook, who supported one employee in transferring a special train from Poland and putting it in a museum.

Sadly, many employees do not realise what could happen to them personally through ongoing corporate changes, despite the evidence around them, and individuals, as such, tend to be neglected by their firms from the personal point of view. It is only when they impact on employees adversely that they realise the full implications, and only then does the employer swing into action with outplacement assistance – but of course it is then too late. Help in re-ordering their lives and careers was needed years before such a traumatic change took place.

We have been involved to a degree in some of the Health Service restructuring, which has provided typical examples of lives and careers that were completely disrupted by organisational change. Faithful employees, who had given of their best for very many years, were moved out of the Health Service through no fault of their own and found themselves (hopefully only temporarily) shattered by the experience, particularly those in their late 40s and 50s. Yet all the signs were there years in advance of the actual change, and each employee could have prepared themselves for this eventuality – but the natural reaction is to say to oneself: 'It will all be all right – they'll surely never get rid of me'. Traditional employees have tended to rely almost completely on the organisation looking after them and guiding their careers, particularly in the public service arena. Fortunately, an awareness of personal responsibility for career progression has grown in recent years, so that, at least for younger people, the practice of preparing for change has developed considerably in recent years.

We suggest that if you are in this situation you might ask yourself the following questions regarding the outcome of current or anticipated organisational changes:

- **What is my next job going to be?**

    ...to which a response might be:'I am more concerned about what the future might hold than about doing my present job well (except in so far as it might influence my future with the firm positively). The job insecurity angle is therefore uppermost in my mind, and I am intent on staking my claim to a future career with the firm. My aim will be to ingratiate myself with those in power and to mark out a short-term career path with them, so that I am able to participate in the changes occurring rather than be excluded by them. I am prepared to work all the hours God sends to achieve this.'

- **How long is my contract for?**

  ...which might stimulate the following: 'Recent moves to modify terms and conditions of employment are regarded with suspicion, and I have to realise that what is set out will actually apply in practice; short-term contracts have become a recognised way of life these days, and I should do what I can to optimise my personal situation. I can no longer rely on the firm to be sympathetic to individual circumstances in difficult times.'

- **How does my pension stack up?**

  ...which might elicit the response: 'I now realise that my pension is a very significant factor in my career, and that I should find out much more about the implications if I were to have to transfer my pension to another firm, or to retire early at 50 or 55. I have little idea at the moment because it has always seemed to be so much in the future. I now appreciate that future financial projections, given different potential scenarios, are extremely important at this stage in my life. I shall also need to work out what my minimum financial commitments amount to so that I shall be aware of the minimum income I need to balance the equation.'

- **How can I make myself more marketable to other firms?**

  Response: 'My capability at present, though strong in its field, is somewhat limited in its relevance outside this firm. What transferable skills do I actually possess? Perhaps I really should consider how I can extend my skills and experience so that I would be more acceptable within this or similar industry sectors in future. I think that I have possibly been misguided in specialising too narrowly in what I am doing at present; it's fine if I stay with the firm, but it could be a handicap if I have to leave or retire early. Perhaps I should consider moving on to a self-employed, contractor basis and take advantage of my specialism by working for more than one firm in the field in which I am established – it would be cheaper for my firm and they might be pleased with such an initiative.'

- **What about the potential impact on my family?**

  ...which might elicit: 'My son and daughter are still at college and it's costing me a bomb. Possibly I should try and set a date in the future when it would be acceptable and feasible for me to branch out on my own, transfer to another firm or "retire" early and change direction. Fortunately my partner has a reasonably stable job at the moment. Even so, I realise that I need to put my mind to this and recognise that this planning should take top priority from now onwards.'

- **How can I live comfortably with this insecurity and risk?**

  Possible response: 'I have to recognise that I will probably never be comfortable with the degree of insecurity and risk that I shall face in my future career years. However, I now value much more than I did before the job that I am currently doing, and the fact that my partner is productively employed. I shall concentrate in the coming years on ensuring that I am more marketable, that I take steps to identify alternative means of employment should I have to leave for whatever reason, and to organise my finances so that I am entirely clear about the outcome of any change in circumstances. I am going to make sure that I control my future career, and will be ready to take the initiative to develop myself as opportunities arise. I am much more confident now, having considered things in some depth, than I was when several people were forced to leave our firm a few months ago; it really shook me then.'

In a recent article by Michael Hanson in the *Evening Standard* on this topic, entitled 'The Disappearing Ladder', he summarises the situation well:

'When the ladder disappears, you will be clinging on for dear life. In the place of a job for life with one employer, you will be looking at fixed-term contracts, temporary employment, studying for additional qualifications, gaining experience wherever you can, changing jobs, even being out of work for periods. It may not be a career as we know it, but it could mean the difference between being employable and being unemployable.'

This subject is covered in greater depth in the management handbook *Employability* by Susan Bloch and Terence Bates (Kogan Page, 1996). They emphasise that employment patterns have changed beyond all recognition, and that careers need to be managed in much the same way as successful businesses; people should assess their strengths and weaknesses, establish strategic goals, develop their assets and market themselves in order to achieve 'lifelong employability'. We concur with these thoughts; however, they are more applicable earlier in a career than in the later stages. It is much more difficult to adapt to a completely different way of life if the career pattern with which you are familiar is based on successfully climbing the ladder in only one or two firms.

The effect of these major changes is illustrated and reinforced by recent research. The 1996 Joseph Rowntree Foundation's report confirms the findings from the Carnegie Inquiry report (1993), stating that there is a very significant proportion of older people, particularly men, who are jobless. The report claims that one in four men aged over 55, and virtually half of men aged over 60, are no longer in work, yet 30 years ago 95per cent of those aged 55 to 59, and 90per cent of those aged 60 to 64, were still economically active. Even 25per cent were in work beyond 65, whereas it is currently less than 10%. This means that expertise is being lost, lives and careers are being impaired, and people are facing 20 years of a healthy life with little or nothing to do. We believe that such a tragic situation needs addressing and the responsibility for ameliorating it lies largely with the individual, which is why we have written this book.

Increasingly there is widespread recognition of the shift from corporations' to individuals' responsibilities for careers and learning. Studies such as the RSA Tomorrow's Company Report and its sequel, the RSA Future of Work project, are promoting a wider debate on the implications of these changes for the individual.

As indicated in Chapter one, for the past century a significant proportion of the population have had their identities, careers and very lives shaped by the concept of employment work. The changes that have taken place over the span of a normal lifetime are quite staggering. They are even more remarkable when viewed in historical context.

In 1750, 95 per cent of the population were self-employed or owner-managers. This figure had reduced to 50 per cent in 1900 and 10 per cent in 1980. By 1990 the figure had risen to 20 per cent again and on present trends will be back at 50 per cent, i.e. 1900 levels early in the next century. So over the same period during which medical science has increased life expectancy by a third, the working population has gone from 50 per cent self-reliance, that is owner-manager or self-employed, to 90 per cent dependence on employment work, and back to 50 per cent self-reliance again. The population now not only lives longer and is therefore required to feed and support itself for that much longer but also, (a) it has to do so from a shrinking employed workforce and moreover, (b) those individuals who are facing this abrupt change in mid-career are the very ones who have become most conditioned to the dependent, employment focused society which peaked in the 1970s and started to decline gradually following the recession of 1979-80, and then accelerated greatly from 1990-91.

In a word, therefore, the impact of corporate change on individuals has been to thrust them to a point where their personal marketability is now the paramount consideration in individual and career survival. This can of course include marketability to other employers for more or less traditional jobs of a quasi career variety. It certainly includes internal as well as external marketability. But above all, it means the individual taking control of and responsibility for his or her own marketability, planning for it, investing in it, managing it and developing it for the future.

The Internal Market

Until a few years ago the very concept of an internal market was not one that occurred to most employees. They saw employers managing their careers according to a plan, even though employers have always had to take a view on the adequacy, or inadequacy, of their internal supply of talent versus the need to go to the external market. The internal market within companies has changed in response to the forces already identified, the shrinking core management cadre, the replacement of clerical hierarchies with technological and systems capability, and the increasing use of specialists and contractors on a contract for services basis rather than an employment contract of service. And of course the massive restructuring, downsizing and re-engineering of corporate enterprises have resulted directly in the departure of large numbers of former employees into the owner-managed, self-employed sector. The internal market is one that employees ignore at their peril and that employers and employees alike must actively monitor and manage continuously.

Employees remaining within the same companies following these extensive organisational changes of recent years have often been made literally to re-apply for their own jobs, an acid test of employability if ever there was one. Those still employed in corporations have also been subject to what we might call survivor syndrome. This is where those left behind can suffer from a kind of post-traumatic shock effect which may be likened in some respects to that experienced by survivors when their colleagues are lost as a result of enemy action in wartime or natural disasters. Unless employers take care to avoid it a sort of siege mentality of fear, distrust, cynicism and shock emerges which inhibits normal professional functioning according to a rational plan.

In his article 'Don't Downsize the Soul of the Organisation Too', referred to at the beginning of this chapter, Howard Davies went on to say:

> 'Organisations that embarked on the delayering process, expecting people down below to share senior management's fervour, have run into problems....they put off reconstructing career programmes for....employees with thwarted ambitions and

morale plummeted. Even those crucial people who stayed are now walking out of the door.'

There are several paradoxes for employers which employees should take into account when planning and organising their own lifeplanning and marketability.

It has long been recognised that while employers believe that they keep the best people when they can, during downsizing exercises a surprising number of employers still find that they lose people they would rather keep as a result of voluntary redundancy schemes. Also, in practice, employers will tend to release the mavericks and misfits first, despite their protestations to the contrary.

Colin Coulson-Thomas, however, points out from his COBRA Study on European Business Process Re-engineering schemes, that it is frequently the unconventional or maverick individuals within companies who are the principal agents of change, thus enabling significant corporate transformation. He pointed out that it is the misfits who get up in the morning believing that the world is a wonderful place and who altruistically set out to make their corporate wellbeing a better one. Such people rather than grand plans and ambitions are actually responsible for securing significant progress in organisational development. However, it is these who are most likely to leave of their own accord if they are not released by their employers already.

The External Market

Here is the opportunity and requirement to test employability in the new labour markets of the emerging post employment society, where what is traded is work to be done and skills to do it but where the parcels of the transaction are contracts for services rather than employment contracts of service: these can be short or fixed term or flexible but the essence of the principal-contractor relationship is that of customer and supplier rather than master and servant.

There has been a paradoxical shift in what employers must do to attract, retain and motivate high-calibre employees. Traditional employment relationships were ones where employers would reward employees for their efforts, sacrifices and achievements today by recognition, promotion and compensation in the future. The instrument of reconciling employer and employee interests was time. Shortterm conflicts of interest between employer and employee were reconciled in the medium to long term because employers controlled career opportunities, and remuneration and reward potential. For those employees who were theoretically able to remain with the current employer, which was most of them, there was no conflict that could not be reconciled and for those who left there was always the argument that it was their choice to leave and had they remained those interests could have been reconciled.

What employers have to do to keep employees now is to maintain their employability. Paradoxically this means that in order to keep staff for longer employers must invest in making it easier for them to go to the external market because for as long as employees feel that they are learning and maintaining their employability and market value then they are likely to stay.

The Institute of Personnel and Development Third Age Interest Group and AMED recently held a conference on 'The Third Age: Change and Opportunity'. In addition to articulating the case for training for flexibility and the opportunities for employers and individuals provided by the ageing workforce, it identified some of the obstacles to Third Age employability in external labour markets and the steps that individuals could take to overcome them.

Reminding us that by the year 2010 there will be more people over fifty than between the ages of 15 and 44, that older workers are less likely to participate in training than any other age group, (Third Age Challenge Trust, December 1995) and that nine out of ten employees aged over 50 receive no training in any one year (Carnegie), John Thompson of Brunel University at the Conference argued that employability depended upon individuals developing a portfolio of transferable skills. He identified five core skill and training fields as follows:

- Career management
- Coaching and mentoring
- Change management
- Networking and contracting
- Internal (and external) consultancy

The Conference also identified the strengths of Third Age workers who provide a pool of talent, skill and experience which in addition to functional competence includes the distinctive breadth and maturity of vision of the Third Agers, together with intuition/sensitivity to events and flexibility, and change management experience – a vital resource for managing innovation.

3

Changes In Mid-Life

We know in our hearts that we are changing as we get older, but we tend to deny the significance of this process unless our faculties actually start to fail or we are brought up sharply by the death of a much younger person. A friend who has recently made the transition from his lifetime career to a post-employment portfolio life emphasised that *he did not feel old* in any way whatsoever. The fact that he mentioned the topic and spoke rather strongly about it tends to suggest that an increasing awareness of one's own mortality does tend to accompany such important life changes. This friend also claimed that he was making considerably more money as well, which possibly accounted for his exuberance!

What happens to us, though, as we progress through life from childhood to adulthood? Is it so straightforward that we start with the First Age – *Education and Growing Up* – proceed to the Second Age – *Parenting and Main Career* – and then move on to the Third Age – *Fulfilment* – which is the important period between the Second Age and the Fourth Age – *Dependency and Decline* – (you know when you've got there, because you will be unable to get out of a chair unaided!)? The concept of the Third Age we find to be helpful, but the entry point to the Third Age is becoming somewhat blurred as the age span during which people make a major career transition is widening dramatically and this can cloud what is happening. Though this book concentrates on lifestyle and career patterns that people may adopt following a main career, we believe that a brief review of different models of life processes that take place as we advance in years would be helpful to our understanding of what is going on, and of the choices available to us in the work and lifestyle fields.

We are therefore attempting to look in straightforward terms at what is happening to us as we move through the age barriers from 40 to 50 and then 60. A very helpful summary of the views of eminent psychologists who have studied these processes has been provided by Diane Salters and Petruska Clarkson ('Metanoia', *Education for Living*, 1988). One of the present authors has found a notable book by Daniel J. Levinson, *The Seasons of a Man's Life* (Ballantine, 1978), to be invaluable personally and professionally with clients at different ages and stages since it was published 20 years ago. It seems to have the effect on everybody who reads it that they recognise themselves and can immediately locate their personal experience in relation to it.

In his book Levinson claims that *mid-life transition* starts at around age 40 and lasts for some five years, though we cannot imagine that this would be the same for everyone. This phase is actually a bridge between early and middle adulthood. The next phase is the *age 50 transition*, which centres around the age 50 hurdle – in today's climate this is probably the age at which you are much less likely to obtain a fresh 'employed' job in the conventional sense, and it is the age from which point the majority of pension schemes allow some form of early retirement to operate. We have known many people who have, either openly or 'between friends', yearned for that day to come! Finally, Levinson sees the *late adult transition* occurring somewhere around ages 60 to 65, which is seen to have more of a spiritual or 'soul' emphasis than the previous transitions.

We believe, as lay people, that it is of practical benefit as well as personal interest for each individual to try to appreciate what these various transitions – which in combination together make up the totality of Third Age transition – are likely to mean to us. There is obviously much more going on within us than we would normally recognise, and the following extracts from the Metanoia model help us to appreciate the main features, which are as follows:

Mid-life transition has the theme *'What am I?'*, and Levinson suggests that we shall be determining the relevance in our lives of four sets of apparently opposed polarities – said to be separate earlier in our lives but becoming more integrated and balanced at this stage of development. The four pairs are:

- **Young** compared with **Old**.

  There is a sense of feeling young, while appreciating that there is a significant element of feeling old as the years pass.

- **Destruction** compared with **Creation**.

  There is a growing acknowledgement that destructive forces are at work in one's life as well as creative ones, with the individual as both a victim and a perpetrator, and that such forces can be overcome by creative acts so as to create things of value that will benefit oneself and others.

- **Masculine** compared with **Feminine**.

  It is generally recognised that we each have a masculine and feminine side to us, and coming to terms with and embracing the other side of us is a feature of this phase, Levinson claims.

- **Attachment** compared with **Separateness**.

  Attachment refers to involvement in the external world, and separateness to the inner world of imagination, fantasy and play. We should recognise the need for both, and for a healthy balance to be maintained between the two.

Every developmental transition, such as this one in mid-life, involves one prevailing life structure giving way to another which replaces it. Though this may seem a somewhat dramatic claim, we can confirm from personal experience that mid-life transition embraces some very significant shifts as these conflicts gradually emerge and are to some extent resolved, though it may be only the start of a growing appreciation of the inner changes which are taking place.

Many people appear outwardly to sail through their mid-life transition relatively smoothly, making the necessary changes they require of themselves and coming to terms with the 'opposites' within themselves without too much pain or turbulence. However, Levinson claims that 80 per cent of men experience a form of moderate or severe crisis during this particular transition. (Gail Sheehy in her book *Passages*, reports similar finding for women.) He indicates that it is a time when every aspect of your life is questioned, though what is revealed may not be entirely to your liking; the main object is to determine a new light at the end of the tunnel, with a new pathway to get there. You might well act somewhat irrationally during this period as you move from one path to another and people might then regard you as 'upset' or 'sick', when this is not necessarily the case. Such a profound reappraisal cannot be a cool, intellectual process, and it hardly surprising that it frequently involves emotional upset, despair and a loss of a sense of belonging until a new pathway becomes clear – and there may be a number of false starts.

An analogy from corporate business life might be relevant here: it is generally recognised that a severe financial or operational crisis can often be a precursor to a period of significant growth and development of the business. The stimulus provided by such a crisis often produces an exceptional burst of creative activity, with positive results, and so it would appear to be the case with our own lives. Mid-life transition – with or without the crisis – therefore presents each one of us with an opportunity for positive change, which is exactly what is at the heart of this book. Levinson is less explicit about what happens during the later stages of middle adulthood, moving through an *age 50 transition* (which he sees as less dramatic and significant) to a transition to late adulthood during the period from ages 60 to 65.

Other experts see the age 50 transition as being more important than Levinson would indicate; Pam Levin in her book *Cycles of Power* (Transpubs, 1980) claims that this age represents a 'particularly active recycling phase' with the theme *'I evolve'*, and the characteristic feature being a reaching inwards to discover what one believes. The authors can support this view; it is an entirely appropriate time for personal and spiritual reflection, for really working out your priorities and determining the values that count for you rather than for the external world.

It is perhaps appropriate at this stage to refer to the views of Carl Gustav Jung, the celebrated Swiss psychiatrist and analyst, to whom we owe the concept of mid-life transition and who introduced the term 'individuation process' – to describe the lifelong process of becoming more uniquely individual, which is the key developmental task of the second half of life. His views link in with those of Levinson, but he saw life being divided into two distinct phases – the first half and the second half, with the dividing line at around age 40. He believed that the first half of life is about developing the *ego* and strengthening the *will* – a phase of initiation into the outward reality or adaptation to external values. The second half of life is about development of the *self* and a phase of initiation into *inward reality*. He claims that personal growth and integration take place mainly in the second half of our lives, and that the first milestone is the confrontation with the 'shadow' side of our unconscious. We ask, *'What is the meaning of life?'* and work through this developmental task in the way indicated by Levinson. Jung highlights the fact that the crossover point at age 40 is very significant in our lives and that we should expect to experience the 'mid-life wobblies' at some stage, which concurs directly with Levinson's findings, including the fact that Jung mentions that the 'wobblies' can start in the mid-30s – you don't have to wait until 40 to throw a few tantrums and blame it on your mid-life condition! Levinson has the 30s transition too.

Then there is the *late adult transition*, which Levinson sees occurring between the ages of 60 and 65. At this stage in life, which should still be very much a continuation of the Third Age, there is a changeover from middle adulthood to late adulthood. Though not characterised by any single event, the way of living is altered in fundamental ways as a result of numerous biological, psychological and social changes.

Levinson refers to the phase from 60 to 85 as 'a distinctive and fulfilling season of life'. It would seem that the move to becoming a mentor, a person with considerable life experience and wisdom, is a prominent feature of this life phase. It represents a distinct change in moving from the 'front line' to a more enabling role, whether this be in the family, or in a work or community situation. Levinson believes that it is important for this generation to realise what is happening so that they don't cling too long to inappropriate roles and become bitter and unloved, rather than fulfilled. This is why we place such emphasis on mid-life planning, which should take into account the priorities of late adulthood in addition to more immediate requirements. For example, if you get involved in, and committed to, a burgeoning new activity in your late fifties, might it not be difficult to extract yourself from that activity (which may depend largely on your personal involvement) in your sixties? We have seen quite a few situations in which the main players have found it very difficult to pass on or sell their small businesses to another generation; planning ahead in an imaginative way might have avoided this.

Our advice, therefore, is to balance your commitments so that no particular involvement in late adulthood will depend disproportionately on you personally. You can be an associate of an organisation, you can even be a chairman or non-executive director, as long as there are others who are bearing the brunt of the activity and you are able to withdraw gracefully should you wish to. We have noticed that the aspirations of colleagues reaching late adulthood change markedly (concurrently with becoming active grandparents, perhaps?) and the desire for exerting themselves at previous energy levels tends to wane somewhat.

What are we to conclude from this brief examination into the psychological changes occurring in mid to late adult life? The authors believe that the main benefit of acquainting ourselves with these considerations is the fact that, regardless of what is happening to us specifically in our personal, family or work situation, we are not alone, there are some common features related to age transitions which will apply as well. If this section helps to achieve such an understanding it will have been well worthwhile.

To take a recent example, a particular colleague was feeling at the end of her tether with her work situation and was contemplating leaving, though she had been in her present job for only a year. She was blaming the stress she was experiencing almost solely on the difficulties she was encountering in her job, and spent a considerable amount of time highlighting the inadequacies of the organisation she was working for. She ignored, however, that she was undergoing a mid-life transition which would have caused a certain disturbance in her feelings in any case. An appreciation of the emotional implications of your movement through the seasons of your life can therefore, we suggest, be a very beneficial input when planning to achieve the level of fulfilment that should be possible.

Let us now look at life transition from a different perspective, from the *Third Age Transition* point of view when, in addition to the psychological changes occurring because of the age we are, a change caused through leaving your main career is imposed on these other factors, the impact of which is experienced more as being indicative of age. We like to emphasise that this transition is about lives *and* careers, not just one or the other, but both. Such a transition will affect every area of your life, because your baseline changes completely; this is particularly the case when you change from an employed to a self-employed situation.

We were talking recently with a senior personnel executive who appeared to be coming through the transition process very buoyantly, and he explained that he had created a partnership of like-minded professionals to join him in a new venture. He also confessed that he had been planning this for a very long while, so that he was able to design an embryonic partnership arrangement and establish appropriate levels of contact with potential partners and clients well in advance of the change – an ostensibly successful Third Age transition for a professional in his 50s. But he is the exception, we have to say.

The majority find the transition process very challenging, as our research described later on will demonstrate; some find it almost intolerable and believe that they no longer have a purpose in life. So why should there be so many differences in the way different people experience the transition? An important factor would appear to be that people in this situation actually have to come face-to-face with their 'real' selves, possibly for the first time since college days, when they used to put the world to rights and then set out on a new life journey involving careers, money and relationships. Ever since that time they have been frantically busy with their jobs, house, family and leisure activities, little dreaming that this way of life might change radically – and for some, without much warning.

One of the questions we put to people who are facing such a transition is to ask: 'What do you believe that you will lose when you leave your main career?' and get them to complete the picture that we refer to as 'The Third Age Iceberg of Loss' (Figures 3.1 and 3.2). Most firms and their departing employees readily acknowledge that the change involves shifts to do with their career and their money matters, but what about all those other features lurking under the surface?

Try it for yourself.

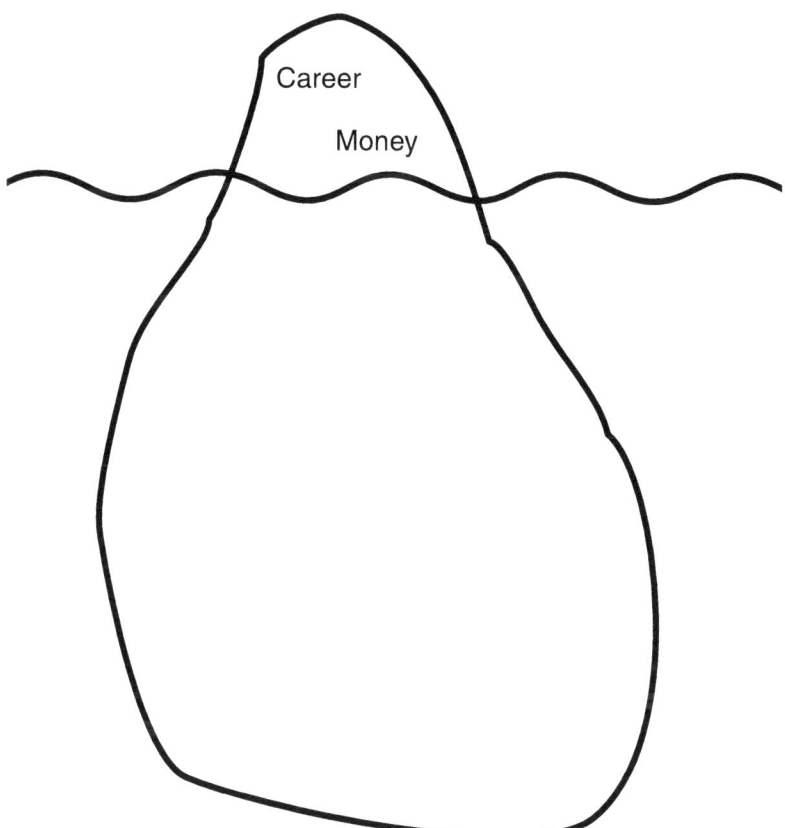

Figure 3.1 The Third Age iceberg of loss on leaving main career

The responses we have had provides a list which is actually quite long! See how many of these you might have missed:

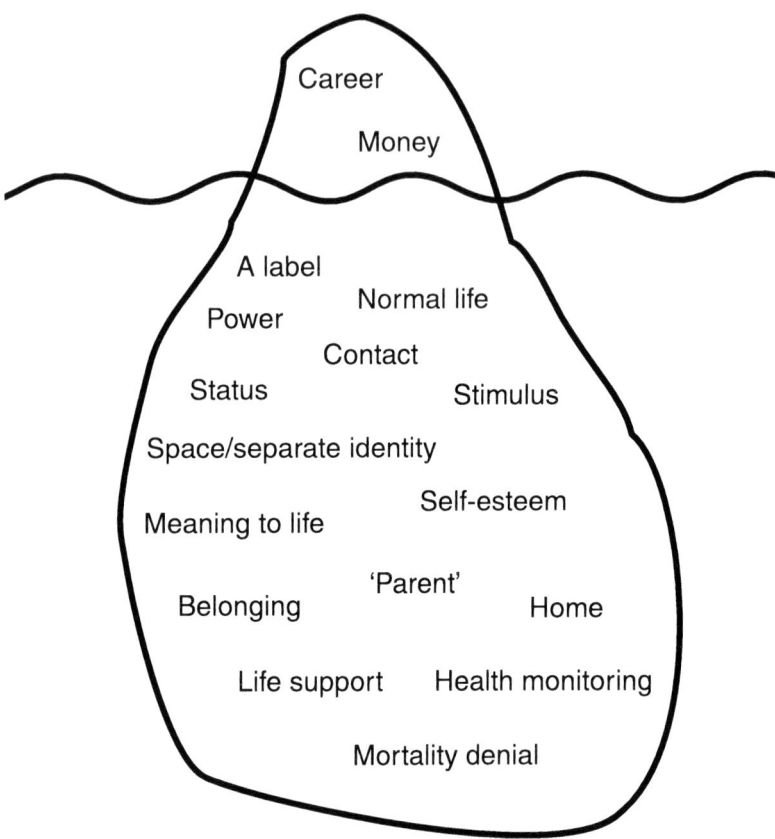

Figure 3.2 The Third Age iceberg of loss on leaving main career (completed)

- **A label,** which tells people who you are
- **Power,** from having a position
- **Status in society,** particularly in own locality
- **Space and separate identity** from partner and family
- **Meaning to life,** purpose in living
- **Belonging to a body,** fulfilling in itself

- **Life support system.** from facilities and people in a firm
- **Denial of mortality,** now being faced
- **A 'normal' life,** from which excluded
- **Regular contact with colleagues, companionship,** seen as 'friends', who then drop you after the change
- **Personal development stimuli,** through being in an organisation
- **Self-esteem**, scorecard of success

and possibly:

- **A caring parent** (if a firm has been paternalistic)
- **One's home** (if it goes with the job)
- **Health monitoring** (if check-ups were funded by the the firm).

How do you feel about these factors? Are they a surprise to you? Do you think that they are 'over the top', and are unlikely to apply to you? Well, each one of these has been experienced to a greater or lesser extent by the people we researched and by the participants in Future Perfect workshops, except for losing one's home, which applies to only a small proportion of professional people. However, all clergy, for example, get thrown out of their homes when they leave their main career – they lose their job, their home, and their network of supportive, local friends. Just think of that if you feel hard done by!

But what about the gains? That is the focus for this book, and dwelling on losses is the last thing that we would advise you to do – though some, sadly, continue to feel neglected by their former organisation and by their peers, which is a recipe for a melancholy and unfulfilled existence. Every transition has its losses, but we believe that, in the case of the Third Age, the gains can significantly outweigh the losses if you get it right, which is what this book aims to help you to do.

So, contrary and opposite to the losses experienced, we have found that 'The Third Age Mountain of Gain' provides a great deal of affirmation and encouragement. Try for yourself to fill in the positive Third Age features that you would expect to experience in the empty diagram indicated (Figure 3.3):

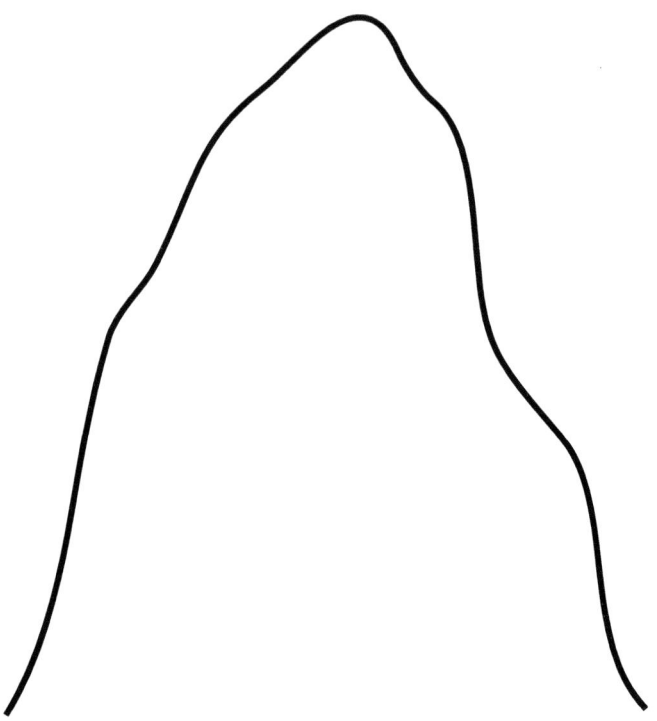

Figure 3.3 The Third Age mountain of gain

Features highlighted by our respondents have included the following:

- **Self-fulfilment**, finding that you are doing things you really want to do
- **Freedom to choose** what you do, when you want to, and with whom
- **More time with family**, a high priority for most
- **New life activities** emerging if you want to change direction, and most do
- **Self-employment**, which provides an income in a different form

- **Opportunity for travel, leisure, hobbies** – never possible before!
- **Time to reflect**, to be rather than to do
- **More flexibility with partner**, working out a new lifestyle
- **Manage your own time**, controlled only by you, rather than a firm's demands
- **Nose to grindstone not obligatory** – you can enjoy life without being crucified!
- **Liberation from past shackles**, being your own boss
- **The chance to read and write** more than before, if you wish.

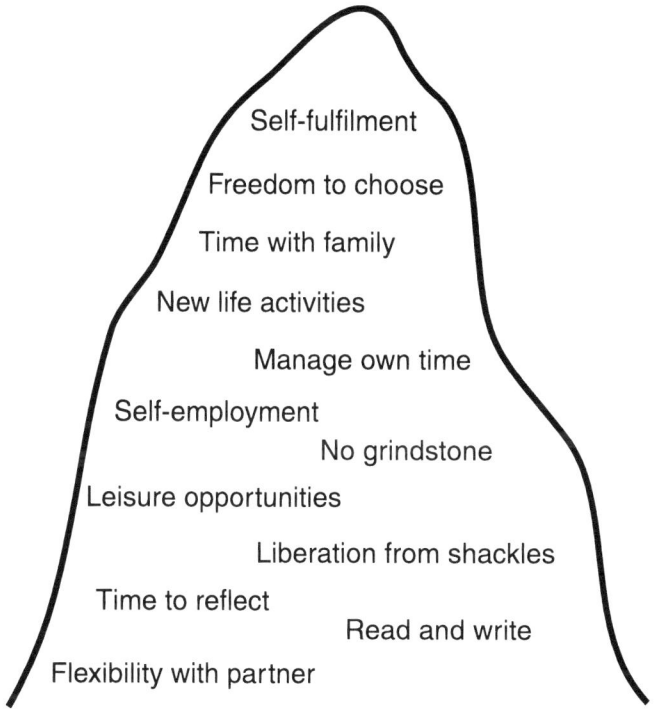

Figure 3.4 The Third Age mountain of gain (completed)

One stark fact that emerges from the above list, however, is that each and every aspect of fulfilment will depend on *you* taking the appropriate action – you cannot rely on anyone doing it for you. This is really the biggest change that you will have to accommodate, since the majority of us tend to rely to a degree on the demands made upon us in the course of employment once we have secured a job. We may have responded actively, but we didn't *initiate* the tasks – they normally arose as part of the ongoing responsibilities of the post; we taught our classes, we managed our unit, we served our clients, but they were to a large extent part of the system which can now carry on without us. After we have left our main career we are very much on our own, and, though the potential for a satisfying life and fulfilling second career is considerable, it does require careful thinking through and planning in advance of the change to ensure that a relatively smooth and successful transition is achieved.

It is encouraging to note the ways in which many older people have flourished in the second half of their lives, frequently doing something quite different. One such example is the best-selling author Mary Wesley, aged 83 in 1996. 'I have no time,' she says, 'for people who don't go on living. People who say "I'm drawing my pension, I'm 69, I'm going to stop." It's a form of mental idleness I think. There's a lot of it about.' In an article about her work entitled 'The rebel who puts love first' it becomes clear that she has poured her life experiences into her books and was first published only at age 70. She delights in mocking the hypocritical mores of the establishment, and considers that love matters more than duty and convention. Her success is quite remarkable, with many of her novels, such as *The Camomile Lawn*, being adapted for television. If she can do that at that age, why not you?

There is also a celebrated collection of senior business executives who have continued their careers until well into their 70s. Examples include Lord Weinstock, who first became Managing Director of GEC in 1963 and only handed over to George Simpson of Lucas in 1996, Tiny Rowland of Lonrho, who, before being forced to leave the company, declared 'At 76, I'm far too young to retire', and John Harvey-Jones, the former Chairman of ICI, who has made a thriving second career in his 70s by acting as a management guru and television troubleshooter.

In other fields Yehudi Menuhin has been as active as ever at 80 in

1996, conducting and recording vigorously, about which he comments: 'We're a family of troopers – my mother's still alive and well at 99!'. George Solti continued to ride a bicycle and conduct orchestras beyond his 80th birthday – he was 84 in 1996. Michael Tippett reached his 90th birthday and Lord Soper celebrated his 90th birthday by preaching in Hyde Park! Famous actors such as John Gielgud, Alec Guinness, John Mills and Edith Evans have all performed strenuous roles in their 80s. Many notable politicians, too, have been elected to high office at an advanced age, such as Winston Churchill and Ronald Reagan, who was 69 when he first became President of the United States.

You may comment that these were uniquely gifted people to whom the normal rules didn't apply, but you might be surprised by the numbers of quite ordinary people who have remained exceptionally active until their later years, well beyond the stereotyped image of the 'older person'. The secret might possibly lie in them all having a reason and a passion for living – if the adrenaline flows then the life usually lasts longer.

The authors both attended a fascinating lecture in 1994 by Joan Reggiori, a psychotherapist at Saint Bartholomew's Hospital, mounted by the British Association of Psychotherapists and entitled 'The Other Side of Fifty'. She quoted Jung as saying: 'The afternoon is just as important as the morning, but different.' Joan Reggiori claimed that the 60s, 70s and even 80s have considerable potential for everyone, but that a stimulus for personal development was needed, this sometimes being provided by the high expectation of others. She pointed out that each person ages differently, and that the inner world interacts with the external world during this ageing process; Jung has emphasised that we become more preoccupied with the inner world and spiritual values. All older people have the young person within them, which most of us would recognise – we don't often feel that different inside from one decade to the next! She concluded by reiterating, and through giving examples, that *positive change is possible* in the therapeutic context the other side of 50. In other words, without the stimulus of a new life and career plan it is possible to succumb to a form of depression; one of the main purposes of this book is to avoid that situation ever occurring.

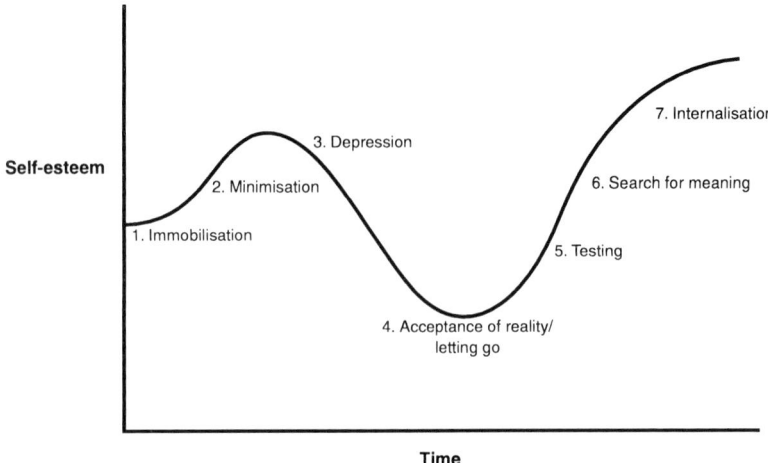

Figure 3.5 Self-esteem changes during transitions

Figure 3.5 traces the pattern of self-esteem that normally occurs during the course of a major transition. The main stages indicated are:

1. **Immobilisation** – when a clear decision is made, or an event leading to a transition occurs, there is frequently a period during which the person is somewhat stultified by something that has not been expected. This is particularly the case with redundancy or enforced retirement.

2. **Minimisation** – a stage when the adverse effects of the transition are denied, and an unsustainable optimism takes over. We have found some people to be euphoric to a quite unrealistic degree during this phase – they have in no way yet come to terms with the implications of their new situation.

3. **Depression** – the false optimism heralds the onset of depression, which can be quite severe. We were told of a senior executive who had a clear idea of what he wanted to do when he left his main career, but had actually completed his list within a year and floundered badly thereafter. There are many, many cases of talented people who have suffered from serious depression as they struggle to accept where they now are in life terms.

4. **Acceptance of reality/Letting go** – there comes a time, however, when it is possible to let go of past glories, to acknowledge without too much regret the losses being experienced, and to welcome the new lifestyle that is replacing the former existence. Having reached the lowest point, people generally make a determined effort to change direction and become more positive, though for some it may represent a gradual and difficult climb out of a pit of despair.

5. **Testing** – a period during which the new, experimental changes are being tried out, in this instance through active consideration of the life and career options already identified.

6. **Search for meaning** – part of the coming to terms with the new situation and adjusting to a different lifestyle is the quest for a rational or spiritual basis for the change, which will eventually mature into a comfortable acceptance of its implications.

7. **Internalisation** – as the climb to a new level of satisfaction and regaining of self-esteem reaches its peak the new situation is internalised and becomes the accepted way of living.

We have found it helpful to explain this process to those involved in a major transition since, to a greater or lesser extent, everyone experiences this pattern of fluctuations in self-esteem. Our purpose in our work, and through this book, is to help people to flatten out the curve and eliminate the depressive trough, which it is quite possible to do. Though there will always be a sense of bereavement for what has been lost, the positive aspects of Third Age living can be a strong incentive for arriving at the new situation swiftly and successfully.

Another perspective on the transition process is given by the American researcher, Gail Sheehy, the author of *Passages* (Bantam Books, 1977) and *Pathfinders* (Bantam Books, 1982). The latter book is based on extensive research in the US, using detailed life history questionnaires and face-to-face interviews with a very wide selection of people, and is geared to finding out what makes for a successful 'pathfinder', someone who takes the initiative to change direction and does it competently. She divides the transition into four main stages, referring to it as the 'anatomy of a passage':

1. **Anticipation** – preparing to meet a transition, based on models of what is possible in the next phase. She highlights the fact that anticipation shapes one's vision of the future, and requires an attitude of flexibility and openness to address the various options that emerge.

2. **Separation and Incubation** – this is the combination of separating oneself from the former life while building up a new one. It involves an acknowledgement of losses being experienced, but also the freedom achieved through a separation from the restriction of the former role and its accompanying set of rules. By way of contrast there is the exhilarating process of reassembling a broader identity and constructing a new life; she highlights the mood swings from depression to euphoria during this phase.

3. **Expansion** – stretching, plunging into new territory, with senses enlivened and insights quickened through choosing to follow our true convictions. New possibilities for personal and moral development present themselves as we try out new ways of responding to people and events. We might even see ourselves as the hero or heroine in our own life story, providing us with the inner strength to build a new life.

4. **Incorporation** – the final phase is one in which we attempt to process what has changed and integrate the meaning of those changes into our philosophy of life. It is a time for our mind to absorb the change and allow batteries to be recharged, taking pleasure in our new personality strengths.

Though these phases are defined somewhat differently, you will note how they follow the same pattern, broadly speaking, of the earlier graph. Both perspectives tend to highlight the benefits of realistic preparation, not necessarily in specific terms but attempting to think ahead and imagine oneself in an unknown future environment. With regard to becoming a successful 'pathfinder' in the future, Gail Sheehy draws attention to the necessary qualities she has observed through her research; they consist of the following:

- **Willingness to risk** – choosing change rather than familiarity.
- **The right timing** – having the foresight to anticipate the future.

- **Capacity for loving** – becoming more sensitive to others, not being alone.
- **Friendship, kinship, support systems** – giving oneself and gaining support in return.
- **Best of male and female strengths** – the man becomes more responsive and nurturing, and the woman more independent and assertive, in the second half of life.
- **A certain age** – the older people tend to be the ones with high well-being.
- **Purpose** – having an identified aim in life about which one feels strongly.
- **Faith** – belief and spiritual expression, arrived at through a variety of stimuli.

Gail Sheehy finds that finding 'meaning and direction' in your life is a critical issue for adult development, and that a high level of well-being can only be sustained if you have a clear purpose beyond yourself. This reinforces the approach that we have developed for life and career development outlined in this book. Each of the above qualities takes a whole chapter to describe in her book; so if you are interested we suggest that you get hold of the book and explore it accordingly! She places great emphasis on achieving a sense of well-being, and has developed a questionnaire to help assess your current situation. We have not reproduced this here because we feel that the majority of our readers would be able to identify for themselves how they would position themselves. It might be helpful, however, just to list the qualities involved as a check list, ranked by her in order of perceived importance:

1. My life has meaning and direction.
2. I have experienced one or more important transitions in my adult years, and I have handled these transitions in an unusual, personal, or creative way.
3. I rarely feel cheated or disappointed by life.
4. I have already attained several of the long-term goals that are important to me.
5. I am pleased with my personal growth and development.
6. I am in love; my partner and I love mutually.

7. I have many friends.
8. I am a cheerful person.
9. I am not thick-skinned or sensitive to criticism.
10. I have no major fears.

So how have you fared out of all that? We would suggest, regardless of how you feel you stand, you should not dwell too much on the outcome but aim to move forward to better things and concentrate on planning a positive life and career ahead. It is helpful, though, to consider which, if any, of the above characteristics you believe should form part of your life objectives in the years to come. Some of them may at first seem somewhat inaccessible and intangible, but, arising from Gail Sheehy's research as they do, would nevertheless appear to represent both some useful enduring truths and not a little wisdom. All of these attributes are covered by a wealth of examples illustrating her findings, and, as such, we commend them to you.

4

Individuals And The Third Age: Perceptions Before The Transition

Factual information about the ways in which people view the prospect of the Third Age, particularly when they 'retire', is scant. There are some theories and models as discussed earlier, but to our knowledge little, if any, research has been carried out on the views and options of mature people who are still in their main career and are approaching a transition in their 40s, 50s or early 60s. Future Perfect therefore commissioned the British Market Research Bureau to carry out a specific piece of research on 'Attitudes to the Third Age' involving some 220 interviews in March 1992.

It is important at the outset to note that people do not appear to think much about retirement or Third Age living until it actually hits them. One Personnel Director confessed that he had felt quite threatened and frightened by a meeting to discuss Third Age transition just one year before he retired; he then started giving some thought to the actual implications for himself. He had forced the topic to remain right at the back of his mind and was denying the very real fear that he had of making this, for him, fateful step. Consequently he viewed the prospect of retirement with dread, so much so that he felt unable to take advantage of the transition support offered to him, because he had barely acknowledged that this change was actually happening, and that it could perhaps be positive.

This aspect, the short time window when people *really* think about retirement or the Third Age, has a considerable bearing on the research findings. One has to appreciate that the bulk of the respondents will not have been in that time window, and will have provided views from their own position of non-involvement at the present time. The responses therefore require careful interpretation, in that they will mostly represent immediate responses rather than considered views.

This 'time window' factor is highlighted when one sees the trauma that sudden, unexpected early retirement brings to many people. We have recently been counselling a successful executive who had just been moved by his firm to a new location and was then asked to retire six months later. Aged 58 (when it could be argued that he should already have been thinking about this prospect), he was completely disorientated by the event. He had been an ongoing achiever, looking to achieve greater things each day, and was the proud possessor of an expensive home with a wonderful family. He, too, had not acknowledged that his main career would end at some stage, and that he had a few questions he would have to ask himself. After a fallow period he began to make decisions about the course his life would take so that he would again, on his own initiative, be an achiever in very different fields.

These two examples illustrate the potential psychological consequences that can occur if Third Age transition is handled badly, either by an employer or by an individual, or indeed not 'handled' at all. We have come to realise that 'retirement' is almost a taboo topic in business circles, rather like death or serious illness, though attitudes are changing as more and more individuals develop their own successful portfolio careers.

1. Importance of Life Features

Respondents were asked to rank five life features in terms of their importance to them at this stage in their lives. The proportion ranking each of the life features as being the most important is shown in the chart (Figure 4.1).

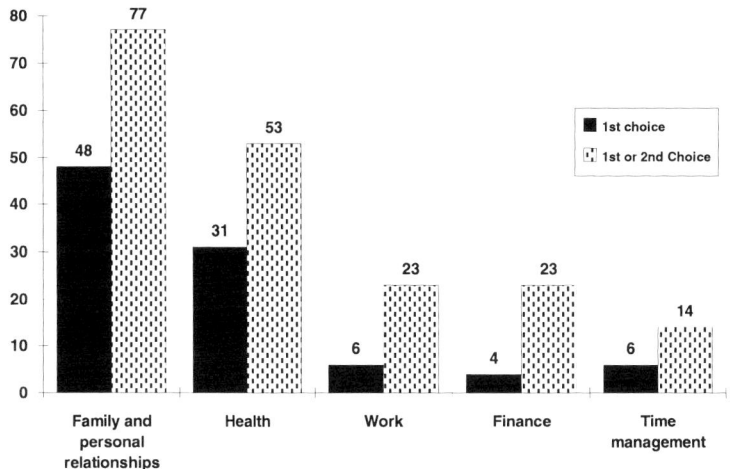

Figure 4.1 Importance of life features

Are there any surprises here? The chart shows a very marked contrast between the first two features and the rest. The extent of the differences is perhaps unexpected, and even more so the way that health appears very prominently in second place. It is hardly surprising that people would generally rate family and personal relationships as a key to their lives, but one might expect health to be more equal with the rest unless there had been a history of ill health, either personally or in the family.

Work and finance come low down the scale in importance terms; these aspects will all now be examined further.

2. Family and Personal Relationships

The vast majority of the sample (85 per cent) were either married or living as married. These people were asked how, following retirement, they expected their relationship to be affected. Figure 4.2 gives their answers.

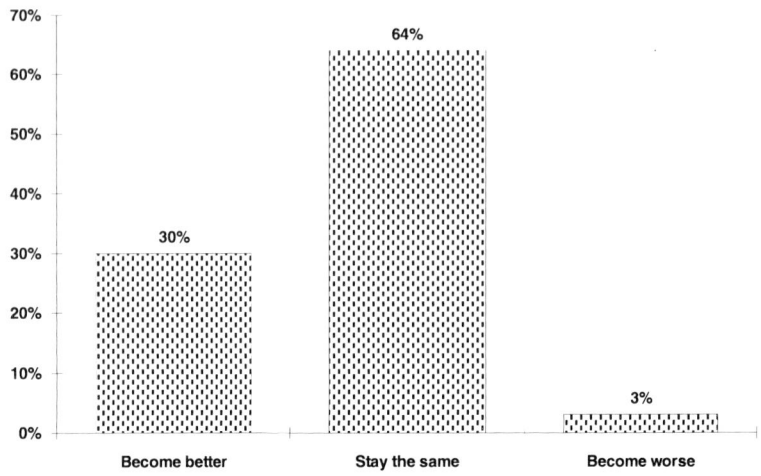

Figure 4.2 Change in relationship with partner

This is an optimistic view of the future! We have known many situations where the period of adjustment following retirement has been fraught, requiring quite a deal of compromise in the life patterns of the partners. However, it is encouraging that such an optimistic outlook is put forward, but we fear that it is somewhat a 'blue sky' approach and possibly unrealistic. We find in our workshops, when couples are drawing up their life plans, that unknown or unacknowledged desires emerge and a considerable amount of negotiation has to take place. It is only when the change is firmly on the horizon that real discussions occur and potential difficulties are appreciated. Most people seem to have a simple image of retirement, frequently one of contentment at not having to work.

In the light of these findings, it is important to consider that every relationship is tested when a major change in life patterns occurs, and this can represent a critical stage in the relationship. Some partners have led very separate lives, particularly the high-powered executive whose wife has had to subordinate her wishes to accommodate the inconvenient demands of her husband. We have seen couples on our workshops where the wife sees herself as a non-person, with nil qualities of her own other than looking after her husband. One such wife had to be ready to deal with her husband at any hour to meet whatever need, because of the nature of his job.

The most hopeful signs are demonstrated when a wife has carved a career pattern of her own, when it becomes more natural for the two lifestyle patterns to dovetail together, and in such situations a positive transition to the Third Age appears to be achieved much more easily. There can be situations, however, where the wife has been so successful at this task that she becomes the really active partner and the husband finds himself in a subsidiary, home-based role. This role reversal can be exceptionally hard for some people to adapt to, which can explain why counselling agencies find that many couples seek help in later life.

Yet our sample, still in the enthusiasm of a pre-retirement existence, assume that their relationship will prosper as they cross the barrier into the Third Age. This can be so, if people intend to be somewhat passive in this phase of their lives, but for those who are active and determined to live life to the full the situation will be anything but straightforward. It is, in effect, similar to the initial stages of the Second Age, when people in their teens or early twenties start on their main career and begin to create a family. We would contend, therefore, that people generally are unprepared for life in the Third Age.

The sample were also asked whether they would be interested in some form of counselling to enrich their personal relationships when they retire. The response was overwhelmingly negative, with 92 per cent being firmly 'not interested' and only 5 per cent claiming to be fairly interested. This highlights the gap between 'needs' and 'wants'.

The main obstacle to participating in some form of involvement would appear to be the conventional British 'stiff upper lip' and fear of anything that is faintly 'psychological'. Yet there is a real need for some form of intervention at critical stages in our lives; marriage preparation or enhancement and Third Age planning probably represent the most significant opportunities in this context. With regard to marriage, for example, the Association for Marriage Enrichment run some excellent workshops, which, despite being directly relevant to a high proportion of marriages, are only few in number each year, in response to a relatively low level of demand.

The lack of openness in dealing with oneself and one's partner seems to be an overriding problem for the current generation; the facade supercedes the reality. Hopefully this will fade as time passes, and our children and grandchildren will demonstrate and accept more genuine views on such important issues.

3. Health

All the participants were asked about their current state of health and were given the opportunity of assessing it as one of four conditions, as indicated in Figure 4.3.

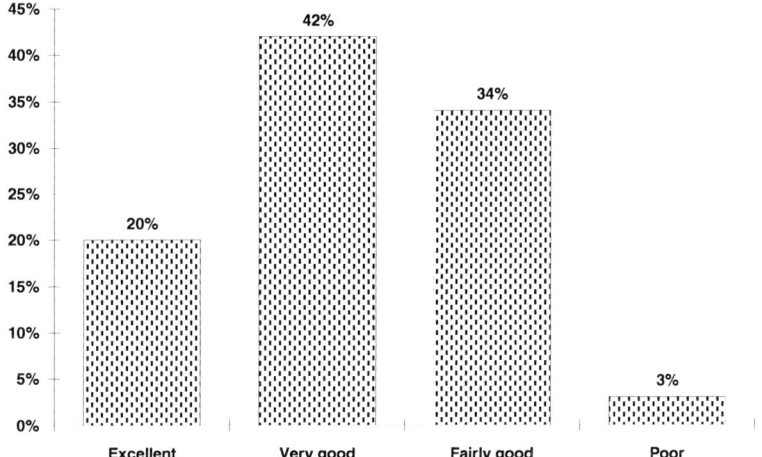

Figure 4.3 Current state of health

Given British understatement, we suppose that 62 per cent believed that they were satisfactory and 37 per cent are less sure about their medical condition. Perhaps of more interest is the incidence of medical health checks carried out. 73 per cent of the sample had medical checks while 26 per cent had not. Of those who had a medical health check 27 per cent had occurred within the last year, 17 per cent 1-2 years ago, 12 per cent 3-4 years ago and it had occurred over 4 years ago for the remaining 17%. From an occupational health point of view, these findings are somewhat disappointing. Surely preventative medicine is about assessing conditions well in advance of any necessary treatment. The older you get the more prone you are to life-threatening ailments. Firms are often prepared to pay for regular medical checks for their senior employees, but what about the needs of the remainder, and the period of time after which they have all retired? The firm may no longer be directly interested in their health, but it would be encouraging if firms, as part of their benefits packages, could do more in this direction, linked to their pension or severance arrangements.

We also asked the participants if they would be interested in having a medical check now. Only 34 per cent would be, if they could afford it. The relevant providers would do well to address this need. An interesting slant on this aspect is that there is a significant difference between those who wish to work after retirement (40 per cent wanting a health check) compared with those who do not (only 25 per cent).

This reinforces the point that many people only value themselves in relationship to 'work'. Their health is surely just as important, regardless of their lifestyle, but the findings conclude otherwise. Even 39 per cent of those who have *never* had a health check are interested in having one now, so this is firmly on the agenda for Third Agers.

4. Work

There was an interesting response to the questions relating to work, which does not appear to rank highly in the overall selection. When asked about certain attributes of work, the features shown in Figure 4.4) were considered to be either extremely or very important:

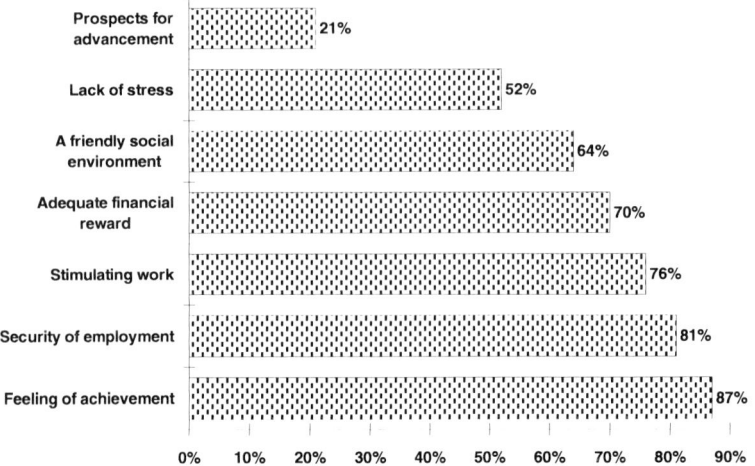

Figure 4.4 Important attributes of work

It is hardly surprising that people in this age group should rate prospects for advancement low, in that promotion frequently ceases to be a reality by the time an employee reaches the age of 50, if not 45, in many organisations. However, the bulk of the rankings appear to be somewhat at odds with the experience of people who have actually retired. What many Third Agers welcome is the lack of stress in their new portfolio careers (compared with their main career, where it is normally high) and miss more than anything else the friendly social environment of being among colleagues who are always there. These two factors (at 52 per cent and 64 per cent) are rated lowly in comparison with the conventional responses of worth-while achievement, security of employment, stimulating work and adequate financial reward. These rather more obvious features, which are rated so highly, are however unlikely to be maintained in the Third Age unless exceptional action is taken by the individual himself or herself.

The underlying implication of the research is that the individual expects his or her employer to deal with all these aspects, which is why security of employment becomes such a prominent feature, for which most of the respondents will be entirely dependent on their employer (who can no longer fulfil earlier expectations). This suggests that the responses, quite naturally, relate as much to Second Age desires as to the Third Age situation, when views invariably change.

In our experience, the quest for worthwhile achievement persists well into the Third Age, and it is this prominent desire which we believe should be encouraged and exploited to the full.

As a comparison with the perceived rankings of importance, the respondents also rated the features in their current situation in a similar way (see Figure 4.5).

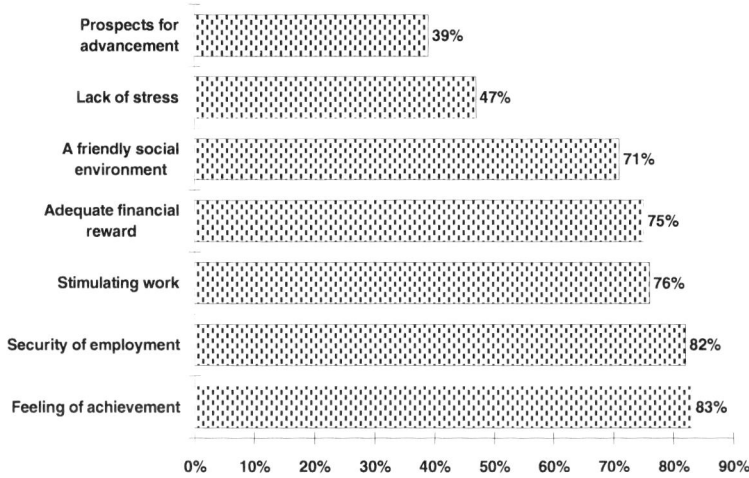

Figure 4.5 Attributes of current position

These rankings tie in directly with the perceived level of importance expressed earlier, which is hardly surprising, though the prospects for advancement appear to merit a much higher satisfaction level (39 per cent instead of 21 per cent), which perhaps demonstrates an over-optimistic view of immediate career development prospects.

In several of our studies we have met fairly typical managers who have felt that they had at least one promotional step in front of them, yet in reality they are candidates for early retirement. If only firms could help to establish more direct communications about future career prospects, a sense of reality rather than fantasy, a great deal of unnecessary distress could be alleviated.

One interviewee in a particular study confessed that he was over-joyed when an application for the next year's season ticket loan was approved; it meant that his immediate future was assured. Should employees have to second-guess their future career in this way?

5. Time Management

The authors of this book have great difficulty in managing their own time, and hence feel very vulnerable in discussing this issue; everyone else is sure to manage their time better! It is something that most of us struggle with in our main career, with a prospect of improvement in the second (though the authors are doubtful of the fulfilment of this projection).

The majority of the interviewees (85 per cent) claim to be satisfied with the way in which their time is currently split between various activities. More than a third (35 per cent) are very satisfied. This is perhaps surprising, and may indicate a relatively modest level of accommodation with life and work. Most busy people seem to find it a continual struggle to get the balance right, and the complacency implicit in the response may demonstrate that certain compromises have been achieved.

6. Age of Retirement

We asked the respondents what they regarded as the 'normal retire-ment' age and also at what age they intended to retire. The responses were very revealing (see Figure 4.6) and are in stark contrast to the reality of the contemporary employment situation.

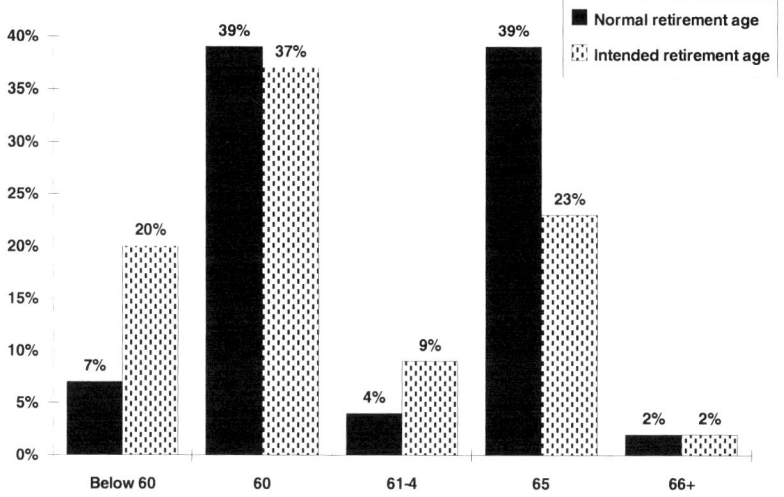

Figure 4.6 Age of retirement

Other surveys indicate that the average age of retirement is now in the mid-fifties, yet only 20 per cent would appear to recognise this fact, whilst 37 per cent indicate their intention to retire at age 60. What about the 34 per cent that intend to retire beyond age 60, though? We suggest that this is quite unrealistic. The sooner people start to plan in mid-life, well before they move on from their main career in their 40s or 50s, the more likely they are to achieve a satis-fying Third Age.

7. Finance

The sample appeared to see finance in some kind of overall life per-spective. When we asked them how adequate their current financial situation was, and what their situation would be likely to be after retirement the response was as shown in Figure 4.7.

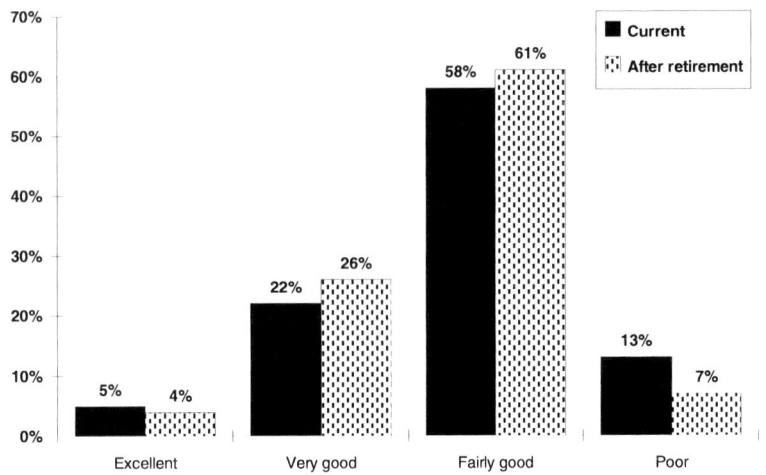

Figure 4.7 Financial circumstances

All respondents were asked whether they had ever had a professional review of their financial arrangements; 49 per cent had done so
(29 per cent within the last year) while 51 per cent had not had a
review of any kind. This is not unsurprising, as many people seem to
live from month to month, ensuring that they are able to meet ongoing
commitments.

The impact of retirement, though, can make a significant difference to earnings levels and one might expect that a review would be
welcomed at this critical juncture. Not so, however, according to our
research. The level of interest in having a review was 12 per cent
interested, 17 per cent not very interested and 71 per cent not at all
interested. This we also find surprising.

There is an undoubted need for professional assistance with an
individual's financial affairs, and participants in Future Perfect workshops consider it a priority. It is interesting to note the caution here
compared with the level of interest expressed for a medical health
check, in which 34 per cent were interested.

8. Attitudes to Retirement

Over half the respondents intended to work following their retirement from their main career: 24 per cent intended to take paid work and 35 per cent wanted to do voluntary work; 11 per cent of the sample wanted to do both paid and voluntary work; 32 per cent had decided that once they retired that was that, enough was enough and they were not going to work again; while 16 per cent were undecided on the matter. Only 5 per cent of those intending to work expected to work full-time; 86 per cent looked to part-time employment to fulfil their needs.

As to the type of work they would go for, the following inclinations emerged:

Table 4.1 Work preferences	
Change to something completely different	47%
In my present field	25%
Change to something slightly different	15%
Don't know	13%
and	
Working for a charity or the community	71%
One or more businesses part-time	25%
Operating as a freelance consultant	15%
Setting up a new business	7%
Don't know	11%

Again there is an overlap, but the findings make interesting reading. They demonstrate that the wish to work after retirement is really quite widespread, at 48 per cent, and that there is a range of intentions expressed, the majority (62 per cent) wishing to do something different and favouring working for a charity or the community (71 per cent).

However, how realistic are these aspirations? Expressed at some distance from retirement they sound plausible, but the moment of truth comes when they have to be put into practice. Ford carried out some interesting research with retirers a few years ago, comparing intentions before retiring with the actual situation one year later. This has revealed a significant shortfall between intentions to work and subsequent success in achieving that situation.

9. Planning for Retirement

We asked the respondents whether or not they had planned their retirement activities. The response is indicated in Figure 4.8.

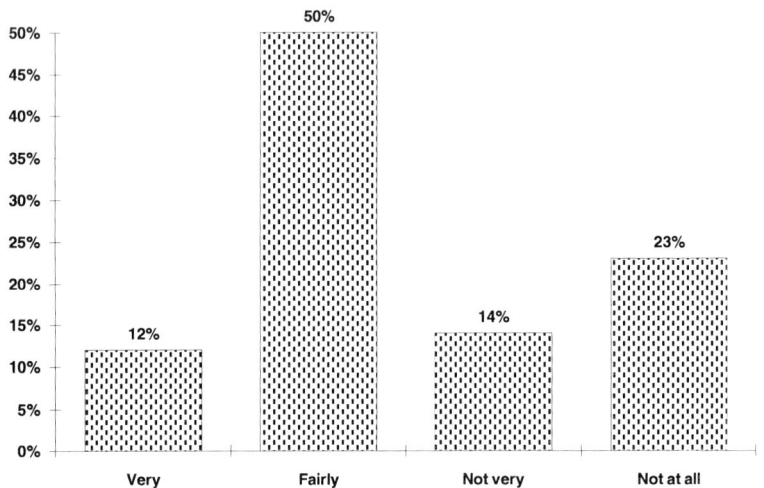

Figure 4.8 Planned for retirement

These findings do not accord with our experience. We can only suppose that 'fairly planned' implies that some general thoughts about the future were held, for example, 'I'll take a part-time job, play golf and spend more time gardening', rather than a substantive plan drawn up.

Our experience shows that when the retirement date becomes imminent, there is often a long period of inaction while the person adjusts to the reality of the situation. There was one lady on one of our workshops who could only write down the date she was leaving the company on her planning sheet; she could not bring herself to think through the implications in practical terms.

We also asked the sample how interested they were in receiving assistance with life planning prior to retirement. Only 22 per cent were interested. Our researchers told us that people appeared to be unfamiliar with the term 'life planning', and that this could be a significant reason for the low response. However, it also illustrates that people try to avoid thinking about their retirement until as late as possible in some cases, the day after the retirement party.

10. Personal Attitudes

We wanted to test people's attitudes to retirement so we asked them whether they agreed or disagreed with some statements that we drew up according to our experiences in workshops. The results are interesting:

Table 4.2 Personal attitudes		
	Agree	
Disagree		
1 I see retirement as an opportunity to relax and do what I want.	89%	7%
2 I see retirement as an opportunity to do something really useful in my life.	59%	32%
3 I would welcome the opportunity for early retirement.	57%	36%
4 I am looking forward to moving on from my current career.	32%	59%
5 I am worried about what I will do	9%	90%

A significant proportion of the respondents welcome early retirement, but at the same time are apprehensive about leaving their current career. This dichotomy is quite understandable, though, and it highlights the difficulty of 'positive early retirement' gaining acceptance as a normal hypothesis. People often find it difficult to be honest with themselves early enough; these particular findings tend to indicate some acknowledgement of the issues involved.

11. Age Discrimination

Most of us believe that age discrimination exists, particularly with regard to employment, but it does not normally affect us unless we are 'old' ourselves. Again we put statements to the sample and asked them whether they agreed with them or not:

Table 4.3 Age discrimination		
	Agree	**Disagree**
1 The older you get the harder it is to get a job	88%	7%
2 I believe a new Government should introduce legislation to prevent discrimination against older people when they are applying for jobs.	66%	25%
3 Society's attitude towards the over 40s is changing for the better	48%	32%

The appeal for legislation from 66 per cent of the sample is significant. Though we ourselves are unconvinced that legislation is necessarily the answer on policy grounds, this seems to represent the strength of feeling on this topic. Attitudes surely have to change on this front, and the positive qualities of mature workers become recognised and valued.

Market and demographic forces – that is, the potential shortage of younger people as the economy eventually recovers – are likely to do as much to change things as anything. Look at the initiatives taken by the retail chains such as B&Q and Tesco. They have been delighted with their experiments in recruiting mature workers, and it is now part of their ongoing culture. We would place emphasis on the growing use of mature people as sub-contractors for given services or projects as the optimum way for the future. Whether or not legislation would assist is a moot point.

We would like to see people assessed on competence regardless of age. One or two companies in our survey observed this practice and the outcome is impressive. Needless to say, however, such organisations have suffered considerable purges before they reached a point where the majority of posts were solely competence-based.

12. Employers' Views

Table 4.4 Employers' views		
	Agree	**Disagree**
1 My company does a lot to help employees prepare for retirement	38%	44%
2 My employer is becoming more negative towards me personally as I move towards retirement	9%	90%
3 My employer would be likely to contribute to life planning services	24%	59%

This demonstrates a number of features. It suggests that mature employees see themselves as being still very much in the fold, and are comfortable with the way that their firm regards them.

This view can change, however, as early retirement beckons or is imposed, and the responses show a distinct proportion who will be unlikely to gain support from their employer in this transition.

The 44 per cent and 59 per cent responses to the first and last statements are not encouraging, and they appear consistent with the findings from other research carried out. One major employer now restricts assistance to the provision of a retirement handbook (because previous pre-retirement events had turned into inappropriate jamborees) and other employers either do nothing or provide a useful short course geared to genuine retirement or withdrawal. We believe that the real needs of individuals are scarcely being met, and who better, partially in their own interests, than the employer to take the lead here. Such practice is evidently beneficial in human resources policy terms; let's hope that progressive improvements will be introduced in this important field.

13. Conclusions

The research reviewed in this section points to a number of conclusions:

- **There is a significant lack of awareness of the Third Age** and its implications and opportunities. Many of the responses appear to reflect 'Second Age' views that are not yet broadened to embrace the Third Age perspective. This 'time window' factor, where the actual span of awareness is currently very limited, is an important feature here.

- **Untapped potential is ready and waiting**, but requires empowering. The population appears to divide itself currently between those who see 'retirement' as withdrawal, and the growing remainder who believe that there may be exciting possibilities for their future lives.

- **Only partly-formed, imprecise views are in place** at this stage. Moving on from one's main career after considerable years of service can be a traumatic experience and merits greater attention.

- **Hence transition support is necessary** to enable people to come to terms with their future state, and be able to plan their lives accordingly. Employers are best placed to provide a framework for this support, which can benefit all parties.

- **It is an important issue for the UK and other European countries** as the number of younger people declines and healthy and active Third Agers become available to make a contribution to the economy. Their active independence should be fostered and harvested. This growing section of the population is probably the most under-utilised resource in the country. It is time that their benefit and worth are appreciated and tapped for the welfare of the individuals, companies and the economy as a whole.

5

Individuals And The Third Age: Perceptions After The Transition

This chapter is based on new, targeted research for this book. We felt that the BMRB research discussed earlier revealed entirely unrealistic aspirations for the Third Age, with the underlying plea from the respondents that it should never happen to them! But we all grow older and there is bound to come a time when we shall have to change our way of life, like it or not. The focus of this book is on how to make the most of the transition, and to prepare for it well in advance to ensure success in whatever field has been chosen, whether it be business, charity, leisure or family.

Who best to find out from than the people who have made the move within the past five years! We have therefore approached a number of known individuals with a detailed questionnaire (see Appendix 3) to obtain relevant information on what appeared to us as being the most important features connected with Third Age transition. In the event, in addition to the wide range of anecdotal and impressionistic input received, we have been able to analyse more systematically the detailed responses from six women and 21 men between the ages of 52 and 66, each having made the transition within the past five years. This has, in our view, been an immensely valuable exercise because of the quality and content of the responses, the depth and authenticity of what they reveal, and the fact that such feed-back is virtually unobtainable from any other source. This particular piece of research we regard as a pioneering activity, and the findings are almost totally at odds with the BMRB findings/perceptions and conventional views. You, the reader, should be able to benefit considerably by absorbing the messages that emerge from these findings, which are set out below in the following sections.

Time Allocation

Though the amount of time spent on business or socially productive activities will vary between men and women, between younger and older Third Agers, it is interesting to observe the patterns that have been established. In terms of main activities the findings can be summarised as follows:

	Women		Men	
Table 5.1 Time allocation (average use of time)				
	Avg	(Max)	Avg	(Max)
Earning				
Consultant/self-employed	21%	(50%)	14%	(50%)
Non-executive appointments	–	–	11%	(40%)
New business activity	–	–	5%	(45%)
Not earning				
Charity/Community/Gift work	28%	(40%)	21%	(45%)
Specific project	1%	(5%)	12%	(50%)
Family/Hobbies/Leisure	50%	(75%)	37%	(75%)
	100%		100%	

Probably the most interesting feature from such statistical findings is not the average, though this reveals a useful guide, but the maximum time allocation that certain people devote to given activities. This is particularly relevant to men, who have frequently chosen a specific project as a focus for their transition – usually related to close personal interests and not necessarily earning any money, indeed quite the reverse in a number of cases where it is costing them significantly. The extent to which people have decided to earn money is perhaps less than one might expect – at 21 per cent for women and 30 per cent for men. Gift and project work comes in at 29 per cent for women and 33 per cent for men, with the balance of 50 per cent and 37 per cent for family, hobbies and leisure respectively. These would be reasonable targets for a new Third Ager to aim at, unless earning money was an overriding concern – but a number of responses demonstrate considerable surprise at how little money they find to be sufficient in this new situation.

Challenges

There are a number of common features to the challenges that our respondents have faced on making their transition. The most pertinent are:

- **Becoming self-employed and working from home**, with the massive changes that this brings in train – particularly the aspect of working alone for significant periods of time, and having to cover every activity oneself.

- **Learning to live without organisational support**, or as one respondent put it, 'without someone to fetch and carry!'. The loss of a secretary or relevant back-up is a bereavement most executives find it exceptionally difficult to come to terms with, and the higher the position the more unsettling the adjustment is likely to be, as those who were chief executives are swift to testify.

- **Earning enough money until drawing a pension at 60** is another common factor; people tend to equate money with self-esteem, and an immediate reduction to zero salary can be very painful to accept (despite lump sums, etc.).

- **Loss of power and influence**, saying good-bye to the big job and all it entails, is something that a good many people find problematic.

- **Interacting with partner's activities**, and avoiding invasion of personal space – applying equally to both partners.

- **Coping with lack of structure** and the change from a high-pressure job involving managing a function to managing only oneself!

- **Greater increase in domestic involvement**, if working from home, is an expectation which many find it difficult to address. Some respond far better than others!

- **Self-confidence to cope with new roles**, and to find work in a field that will adequately use one's experience and professional skills.

- **Empty nest, ageing parents and moving house** – all factors in the Third Age transition for some. 'Living on a boat' was one specific challenge quoted also!

Help Obtained from One's Organisation

It is remarkable that so few of our respondents felt that their firms could have done more to assist with their transition, yet, for the majority, their firms had done precisely nothing! The positive help that had been initiated by the employing organisations included the following:

- **Sending both partners on a Future Perfect or pre-retirement course.** It was gratifying to note one comment: 'They sent me on a Future Perfect course, which was excellent, and on their own Retirement course, which was useless.' Undoubtedly an appropriate Counselling and Information intervention at such a critical life and career stage is seen to be beneficial – one person claimed the effect to be seminal – but few employers seem to appreciate the implications and genuine requirements. The sad feature is that those who have not experienced appropriate support in this form will not appreciate how beneficial it could have been; this applies to people who went on a superficial or 'jolly' type of course as well as those who went to nothing.

- **Providing continuing part-time work.** This was seen to be of great benefit for the relatively small proportion of participants that experienced it. The extent involved varied considerably – from 40 days of consultancy to a 2½ year retainer! In our view very much more could be made of the skills and experience of mature employees that is available in this way. One respondent commented that he appeared to be both regarded more highly and paid more money as a part-time consultant than when he was actually an employee! When it works well it seems to be mutually beneficial to a high degree.

- **Agreeing a specific lead-time.** One executive mentioned that one of the secrets of his successful transition was the 18 months lead-time negotiated with his firm. The problem is that few people are sufficiently confident – and few firms sufficiently courageous – to raise such an issue so far in advance. One Board we came across was not even prepared to discuss the issue of executive retirement at all, so how one could negotiate imaginatively with such an organisation is a little problematical. The period could, of course, take the form of a paid 'sabbatical', which was the case with one of our respondents. Another said he had been planning since age 44, but we do not believe that his firm realised that that was the case!

What Is Most Enjoyed About Current Portfolios?

It is encouraging to note the way in which people have responded so enthusiastically about what they now enjoy most. Though there are inevitably different emphases, the following extracts demonstrate a common view in many cases:

- **Freedom.** 'Doing what I want how I want and when I want' is how one person expressed it. Freedom to choose in this way, particularly regarding use of time, is seen to be the top benefit to be obtained through this new lifestyle – it is referred to either directly or by implication by almost all of our respondents. One person emphasises the benefits of 'a lack of commuting' in this context, in being able to choose to travel to London during off-peak times in certain instances; working from home and avoiding the travel crushes (clients permitting) is a treasured benefit for one of the authors.

- **Variety of experience.** A former CEO puts it well – 'The experience of learning about and fitting in with a number of very different working environments and cultures has been tremendously stimulating. The variety that this has brought has introduced a dimension with work that a lifetime career with my firm could not provide.' There are countless testimonies to this effect, which is why, on Future Perfect programmes, we always attempt to encourage people to think imaginatively about all the possible avenues that they might take, even if they seem ridiculous at that stage. We know from the feed-back we get that it is actually stepping out into the unknown and experiencing new challenges that is so very beneficial – it really does enable one 'to live more than once', because the experience is so different from what one has been used to.

- **Meeting new people.** We have always felt that business people tend to live somewhat narrow lives, and are only really comfortable with conventional paradigms. They are familiar with organisations and organisational behaviour – even if, by doing something outrageous like wearing bright red braces, they might occasionally break the mould. Many business people have experienced only one business sector during their main career and appear to be less comfortable in other working environments (particularly where formal clothes are not worn!). One of the authors is still trying to adjust to colleagues in a new environment where crew cuts and body piercing are almost de rigueur, to say nothing of the multifarious and multi coloured garments that impact unharmoniously on the visual senses. It is indeed fascinating to meet new people, especially when they are from totally different cultures or working environments.

- **Travelling.** Undoubtedly travel to other countries can be extremely attractive, especially if you can be paid at the same time. Several of our respondents have in fact managed to achieve this, and one former civil servant now refuses to accept overseas assignments unless he is both paid and is given sufficient remuneration to be able to take his wife with him. Another person has highlighted 'living in France' as something he and his wife have most enjoyed, and few would disagree, we are sure, given the opportunity. They, however, have made the opportunity – no one told them to do it, and they chose freely!

What Is Missed

Strangely there do not appear to be strong views on what is missed from a main career lasting many years – most have moved on beyond that. What people will admit to, however, is nearly always the same and can be summarised very easily:

*   **Colleagues, peer group.** The authors concur with respondents in missing the stimulus provided by the ongoing interaction with business colleagues that one has known and worked with for a number of years. They are often more than colleagues, and as well as providing companionship, they offer the rapport and challenge that is so beneficial when considering new projects or ventures. It is our view that new networks are necessary for people to flourish in a new, portfolio environment to counteract this loss.

*   **Administrative support.** Virtually *everyone* found that the lack of administrative support was the unwelcome face of their new existence, but most accepted this aspect stoically. Some even appeared to thrive on becoming a self-taught computer buff, and were able to reel off the various programs that they were abreast of and the desk-top publishing achievements that had been realised in recent months. A number had bought administrative assistance rather than do everything themselves, but had found this a less than satisfactory experience on the whole. The answer would appear to lie in streamlining what is essential, and limiting activities to what is necessary rather than what is desirable.

The above represented the majority conclusions, but a few were brave enough to confess that they actually missed the *money* that went with their main career, and there was a view that overseas travel and those various company get-togethers in foreign parts were probably appreciated much more than was recognised at the time. One person claimed that what he missed, very positively, was not having a boss!

On the topics of *money*, *age of transition* and *possible regrets* the responses were very muted. The majority found that they had enough money for their needs, that the best age for moving on from a main career was between 50 and 55, and that there were very few regrets – most were emphatically positive about their current lifestyle, including those who had to run fast to keep up with their financial demands. It seems that we are more adaptable than we might have imagined.

Partner's Views

It is probably best for us to list typical responses, in abbreviated form, which tend to vary widely but will each have their own relevance:

- Happier
- More sharing
- Positive help to renegotiate relationship
- Accompanies on all travel
- Enjoys it as much as I do
- Seen less of him than expected
- Talk out feelings and problems
- Communicate feelings, and have action plan
- We have grown closer
- Had to dovetail activities for time together
- Get out together, domestic boundaries adjusted
- Foreign students take up time
- Hope to do more together, but concerned to respect each other's activities
- Enjoys seeing more of me
- Move to country, more challenges
- Freedom restricted somewhat
- Find it difficult to combine portfolios
- Welcomes domestic support
- Been supportive and tolerant
- Enjoys having me around, but dislikes absences abroad
- More help domestically
- 'House husband' tasks carried out
- Missed contact with firm, moved house also.

These comments, though somewhat curt, are on the whole very positive and help to identify the areas that anyone planning to make the move should consider. Don't forget that the above responses come from a mixture of men and women, generally with their own portfolios or working careers.

What Has Been Surprising

The comments on this topic have overlapped to a degree with the responses regarding features which people have most enjoyed. However, we believe that it is worthwhile to record at some length the particular aspects which have genuinely surprised people taking 'a step in the dark'. The most notable comments included the following:

- Easier to say 'no' to former level of work.
- Happier vision of life possibilities.
- Minimal withdrawal symptoms – relief from pressures.
- Easy to make money as a consultant! Importance and benefit of networking.
- Took longer to make complete change than expected – four years.
- Usefulness of capability to developing countries – exciting and self-enhancing.
- Not missing in the slightest business/big numbers.
- A lot less time for writing than planned – should be 60-70 per cent.
- Partner not 'under feet', but more in tandem.
- Need much less money than expected.
- Broke the (main career) psychological and work contracts easily.
- Positive approach to opportunities.
- How quickly one can settle into a new regime.
- How much my wife and I have enjoyed the past four years.
- So easy to drop professional life; how long everything takes but it doesn't matter!
- Becoming a successful teacher of English and French; interesting, varied and very rewarding.
- How much I enjoy the voluntary sector; helping others is satisfying, interesting and rewarding.
- Adapting so easily!

- The need to chronicle each day's events and achievements.
- That I seem to be valued more as a personnel consultant than as an employee!
- High energy level, determination to keep going, freedom, and control of life.
- Freedom in deciding own timetable.
- My contentment.
- Greater awareness of nature and seasons.
- Time consumed by admin for travel arrangements.
- Greater self-confidence and enjoyment of life; regret at not having been calmer for children.
- Greater control over working time.
- Different nature of responsibilities and accountabilities in the absence of a hierarchy.
- Synergy across differing roles.

This represents a fascinating snapshot of personal responses to elements of transition which have been unexpected, and they provide us with some insight into the features of life which appear to be significant – in our view most of the above reactions could apply to anyone experiencing this major mid-life transition.

View of the Future

Again we believe it would be interesting and helpful to quote a number of the personal responses about prospects for their future lives:

- 'I worry about work and professional interests, but time and hobbies are a just reward. I worry too about health and ageing; I am careful with money, but 1000 per cent happier.'

- 'It's too good to be true! I have a broader spread of activities, but work only 65 to 70 per cent and spend balance with my partner; marriage is most important. Health, too, is critical'

- 'I just bicycle to work and get on with it! It feels OK.'

- 'I wish to continue working for my major client as long as they and my health allow. I feel good.'

- 'I hope to retain health/fitness by climbing (Alps and Himalayas) and sailing (Atlantic). My happiness has always been under-pinned by health, wealth and satisfying work with congenial colleagues. It still is. Long may it last.'

- 'I'm very optimistic. Health good, no money worries, never liked work, hope to write more. High rating for happiness.'

- 'The future is bright, based on *family*. I want to live and die well, to be at peace with myself and with my soul.'

- 'I am optimistic – my main fears are about health. I want enough time to do things together with my partner.'

- 'I want to see my grandchildren mature. I fear being left on my own – I live one day at a time. Working for the good of others brings happiness – the love of money unhappiness.'

- 'I shall hope to continue as now – I am happier now than I have ever been.'

- 'I'm excited at making the change, but might take on too much. Health, wealth and work is fine, but the transition is stressful – happy home and family, though.'

- 'I intend to reduce my commitments and relax more. I'm happy to live on my pension and ease off the work load – three children will be married off by the year end.'

- 'I look forward positively and with excitement; I want to add to my range of activities. I'm healthier and happier, but my wealth is affected by our new house!'

- 'I feel good. I hope to continue as is, but I'm aware of dating of skills. I need to learn to enjoy relaxing, to make full use of my time, be active and enjoy people.'

- 'Positively, but I want to achieve higher fee levels and more spare time. Happiness is most vital, but difficult if both partners are working/living at home.'

- 'With pleasure! My ambition is to raise the level of academic quality of the museum (which is my voluntary, second career). Health plus Wealth equals Happiness, of which work is a happy outcome.'

- 'My hopes/objectives are to continue in a similar way, adjusting in time to ending work – I have a good enough balance at present.'

- 'I plan to give up consulting work at age 65. I have a master plan for my garden (one acre). I am content, but my partner does not enjoy good health.'

- 'With enthusiasm. Arts therapy is my main interest and ambition, also working with children and enjoying my grandson. I plan to continue working for a long time – both my pension and my grandchildren will benefit!'

- 'I shall adjust my portfolio to step down gently into retirement and time it with my wife's needs. I believe that God will guide me in this, and health, wealth, work and happiness will flow from that.'

- 'There are two phases – I shall need to prepare for retiring all over again, and I look forward to further adjustments. I aim to avoid being a burden to the family later on.'

... a fascinating diversity of views, we are sure you will agree.

At this stage in the book we feel that we should add some observations of our own which have arisen from discussions with the research participants. We have noticed, in both ourselves and others, that there is a tendency for people to progress through a number of distinct phases once they have left their main career. Though they will move almost imperceptibly from one phase to the next there are some identifiable characteristics and patterns in each phase that people have acknowledged when the hypothesis is put to them. In planning ahead we have found it beneficial for this concept of phasing to be appreciated, so that you will be able to realise that any plans made are not cast in stone and should be approached flexibly.

The norm would appear to be represented by the following three phases, the length of which will be influenced by the age at which the initial transition takes place, but we are talking about years rather than months:

Phase One: Adjustment and Consuming Activity

The period immediately following the transition will affect different people in different ways, but the majority tend to combine some form of holiday or relaxing activity initially with their main preoccupation of attempting to engage in a completely different lifestyle and new career role. This new career role, whatever it may consist of, is soon likely to take up a very significant proportion of your time, and for many it becomes all-consuming. Though the level of activity for many will be slightly less than before, there are many for whom it will be very much greater, particularly for those starting up in some form of business activity on their own or with others.

From our perspective it would seem that people during this phase are essentially seeking to replicate the earnings and activity levels that they have been used to in their main career. It is in part subconscious, because it is difficult to reject the habits of a lifetime (not quite, but it might seem like it), and self-esteem may also lie at the root of the motivation in this phase. Everyone wants to be seen to be successful, and it is really considered in effect to be a time of testing to demonstrate that leaving one's main career has been merely a step to better things – and the image of successful achievement will have been preserved. Both the authors can be included in this category, and we have noticed exceptionally high energy levels being exerted by many professional people to achieve these objectives. Sometimes this becomes visible through declared earnings achievements (normally not talked about), expensive accoutrements (such as cars and houses), costly receptions and celebrations (not a bad idea for the guests) and a host of other indiscreet boastings. Such an intense lifestyle is likely to be quite stressful, however (possibly damaging to health and family relationships), and it is prudent to be conscious of the most appropriate time to move on to the next phase.

Phase Two: Balancing the Lifestyle

The next phase emerges when you have had the chance to reflect on the frenetic activity that has occurred during Phase One, regardless of the perceived level of success involved. If successful you may start to ask yourself: 'OK. I've made a success of things, but do I really want to carry on working like a lunatic for ever?' or, if unsuccessful: 'I've tried hard and found it a valuable experience – I don't regret a minute of it – but do I really want to carry on any longer flogging a dead horse?'. So you gradually come to the realisation that new criteria need to be applied to your working life, and most people come to a firm conclusion that they will take on *only those projects or activities that I really want to carry out*. For example, one of our participants is involved with overseas projects and he now sets the following parameters as a condition for accepting an invitation to carry out a project:

- It has to be in a country which is of appeal to him, living under reasonably attractive conditions.
- The timing has to suit his diary (and presumably be between given duration limits).
- He is able to take his partner with him.
- The financial terms and conditions have to be acceptable.

This means that he has reached a point at which he is entirely self-confident about his worth, and that different priorities have emerged now that he has had several years of establishing himself in that particular role. If money were the main criterion he could no doubt be operating virtually full-time on various overseas projects, but he has now seen his life and career in a new light. This is unlikely to have manifested itself as a shattering revelation, though there are often occurrences that appear to be the last straw when you say: 'Well, I'm blowed if I shall ever do *that* again – after all, I have complete freedom of choice.' The portfolio is therefore adjusted to suit a more relaxed set of priorities, and it may even involve something completely new – but about which you feel very strongly. The ability to say 'NO' becomes essential at this time, if it hasn't done so already. This phase is also likely to include a greater emphasis on taking adventurous holidays, and possibly doing things that are new and stimulating in the leisure and artistic field that haven't been practicable earlier on.

Phase Three: Living a Comfortable Life

This third phase doesn't necessarily imply a reduction in energy or activity levels, but it involves a subtle change in perception of your own lifestyle. A colleague made the point to us recently by declaring 'I reckon that I've retired now!'. He knew that this statement would upset us, because we don't believe that there is any such thing as retirement, but what he meant was that, as far as 'work' was concerned, he had settled down to holding one or two non-executive directorships, had stopped going actively after clients, and would respond only to specific requests for consultancy assistance that were of appeal. He had adjusted his financial situation so that he was able to live comfortably without having to work so hard, though the observed energy level appeared to be much the same as before!

For those on a reasonable pension level (possibly one from a main career plus an addition for a second career) it should be quite feasible to stop all savings or new investment activity, and to draw a greater proportion of income than before from the yield of existing investments. For a professional person in their 60s or 70s, which we suggest to be the appropriate age range for reaching this phase, it should be entirely feasible to live reasonably well without the need for additional, earned income. That doesn't imply that earning money isn't appropriate within this phase, because it may well be an integral part of doing what you really enjoy; psychotherapy and counselling, for example, includes practitioners of quite advanced ages since the experience and wisdom gained in a long career is much valued by clients and agencies alike.

There appear to us to be these three phases, therefore, characterised by hard work and earning money in Phase One (during ages up to the mid/late 50s), getting things into proportion in Phase Two (from mid/late 50s to early/mid 60s), and relaxing a little more in Phase Three (from early/mid 60s). We suggest that being aware of this potential progression through the phases is extremely helpful at the initial Third Age planning stage. It means, in practical terms, that you don't have to do everything at once, and that you can genuinely afford to put a desirable project on the backburner for a few years – it need not be discarded.

6

Advice To Give To A Younger Colleague Approaching A Move From Their Main Career

One of the most valuable outputs from this recent research – if not the most valuable part of this book for anyone approaching this transition in the immediate future – is the advice set out so thoughtfully and succinctly by the participants. In our view these statements are incredibly powerful, being based on on directly relevant experience. Each statement has its own emphasis, and we are therefore recording a considerable number of those we received to provide as comprehensive a picture as possible, as set out below:

- 'Don't rush. Give yourself time to think why you are changing. Get in touch with what you really feel strongly about. Talk to people and let the ideas marinate. Experiment; it's OK to change your mind. You don't have to justify what you are doing to anyone but yourself. Share hopes and fears with your partner as honestly as possible. Go for it and good luck.'

- 'Plan carefully over several years, i.e. do not just plan for the immediate but devise a plan that fits with your own changing needs and hopes over at least five years. Beware of promises (work-related) that disappear. Be prepared for quick changes in direction and remember that negative thought gets you nowhere whereas positive thought gives you energy.'

- 'If possible, do it bit by bit. Don't rush at it, try to "listen to your guts" for when the time is right. Do plenty of research, wait and trust that any muddle will clarify and you will see a way ahead.'

- 'You will have a need for intellectual stimulation and creativity, quite apart from any physical activity. Think seriously now about which avenues to explore – then start exploring. The longer you prepare, the easier the transition. Aim to become financially independent, to give you freedom of choice. Keep a watch on your current health – it is an essential investment. Plan the future with your partner; to help them in the transition they need to be confident about their role, too.'

- 'If you are considering a portfolio career, please:
  1. Speak to two or three people who made the decision some three years ago – listen to their successes and failures and learn from them.
  2. Learn how to run a small business before you go too far down the portfolio road, e.g. VAT, accounts, tax.
  3. Ensure you produce a different CV with achievements clearly identified and focus your time and energy within one hour of your home/workplace.'
  4. Ensure that you have at least three and no more than six income sources.'

- 'I am reluctant to offer advice; how one lives and what one enjoys is a personal matter and individual choices differ greatly. In my own case I have derived great pleasure from practising the skills developed in my main career, offering continued mental challenge. Beyond that, being physically active and participating in competitive sport with other people has given both pleasure and wellbeing. A balance of intellectual challenge, physical activity and the company of others is a good recipe for the Third Age.'

- 'Ensure that you explore every aspect of help offered by your employer, taking advantage of outplacement guidance, financial counselling, etc. Remain on good terms with your erstwhile employer and colleagues but remember that you will no longer be relevant to their daily business. Regard any transitional period as very precious time to be used wisely and fully in preparing for the future.'

- 'Carefully assess your strengths and weaknesses (make a hit). Think about what you *really want to do* (even if it is a long way from your current role) but *be realistic*! Consider your partner, more than most of us do! Talk to your employer if you feel able – be bold – he may come up with a solution (e.g. part-time role,etc.). Get help with the financial aspects if you need to.'

- 'For any wife and mother who gave up a career to care for a family and/or to support a husband with a demanding job, I would recommend developing interests, finding part-time employment, or getting involved in charitable work. It is very important to retain flexibility in anything one takes on so as to be able to combine any new employment/interests with the existing role within the family. It is also important that husband and family back you 100 per cent in your new role(s), so discuss your plans with them first.'

- 'Take this change as an opportunity to rethink your life. Does this provide you with the possibility of starting another career path? What are the things that you would like to leave behind (perhaps commuting?) to provide a way for you to see more of your family and improve the quality of your life? Share your worries and dreams with your partner; two heads might be better than one. If you are making a major decision, get the best advice you can; this might avoid seeing the next move through rose-coloured spectacles. Do not forget to count all your strengths. It is easy to lose faith if things aren't going right. If circumstances permit get your priorities right. Health, contentment and happiness are more valuable than money, property, shares, etc., although we know that you can't live on fresh air. All this may sound very pious, but if you don't think through your philosophy of life at this time you may not get another chance.'

- 'Think through what you want to do (e.g. extension of present work, new areas of work using your skills, study, etc.). Plan your finances to the appropriate course of action you take. Keep your partner informed, consult your colleagues about opportunities and how they see your skills, etc. Build networks of contacts in the areas you are interested in. Be open with the company about your ideas and proposals – good ones will help you. Be positive – it's a great opportunity. Look forward to the freedom.'

- 'Clear your debts, although you can live on far less money than you think. Cultivate your mind, your interests, your soul. If you need to work for self-esteem and to meet people, go voluntary – or travel, become a courier (if no family ties), or go abroad on a shoestring, learn about the world. If you need money, make something of your *interests*, not only of your experience.'

- 'You need to start thinking actively, as early as you can make yourself, about what you *really* want to do. If the answer is, "This job for as long as I possibly can," it will be prudent to consider, "But what if this job doesn't want me?". The key is: always be in control of your career. You give surprises to others, perhaps – but don't let yourself be surprised and lose control.'

- 'Do not allow your main career to so overload you that you have no time for other strands in your life (in all my adult life I have been an active sailor, mountaineer and painter).'

- 'Do not underestimate the experience and skills you have acquired. Although it may be necessary to adjust to a new environment and in some ways to start afresh, a realistic review of your successes in your career so far should give you confidence to tackle what lies ahead.'

- 'If you need the money, go out and get another job quickly. If you don't need the money then take the time (deliberately) and see if your priorities (money, status, family balance) are the same after a year – they may be surprisingly different. Check your health is OK and, if not, do something about it. Be honest with your family – sounds easy but it isn't.'

- 'Involve your partner in the planning of the transition, particularly on the implications for his/her lifestyle. Decide how much money, if any, you need to earn and set objectives accordingly. This will tell you how much time you will have for charitable/educational/

sporting/family (i.e. non-paid) activities. Network as extensively as possible in your areas of interest; tell people as early as possible about your plans. Organise a separate room at home with fax, computer, etc., so that you can have your own space (and can give your partner space) as well as organise, file, correspond, etc. It really isn't scary out there if you plan realistically.'

- 'Decide the phases you and your partner want to have in life, and make them happen.'

- 'You must look at this as an opportunity. Put aside any thoughts of past regrets. Look only forward, using the skills, knowledge and wisdom you have acquired. Be confident in your past achievements but speak only modestly of them. Be courageous and take sensible risks. Be positive at all times and let the enjoyment show through. Delight in other people's success, particularly those you are helping to develop and coach.'

- '1. Start thinking well in advance what you would like to do and be very objective about whether or not this is achievable.
  2. Plan your finances very carefully – make sure the sums add up.
  3. Involve your partner fully in planning and thinking about transition.'

We hope you will agree that the above statements are extremely interesting and helpful; the variety of emphasis and depth of insight has great appeal, we believe. It is perhaps surprising that no participant has attempted to try to persuade a younger person to pursue a particular course of action regarding choice of activity – they have all confined their remarks to a view of priorities, as observed from recent experience. We have therefore tried to draw together those priority features to provide a succinct, composite picture of what are considered to be the beneficial steps to cover in the transition process:

- **Develop other interests** as early as possible alongside your main career.
- **Think about the change** long before it is likely to happen.
- **Remain in control** of your own career.
- **Don't rush** – take time to mull things over.

- **Involve your partner** closely.
- **Assess your capabilities** realistically – don't underestimate them.
- **Work out your financial situation** carefully – get advice if necessary.
- **Decide balance of paid/non-paid work** that would be appropriate.
- **Identify a vision** for the future.
- **Choose priority wants.**
- **Plan and prepare well in advance.**
- **Network extensively** in particular areas of interest.
- **Establish a home office** or separate study room.
- **Watch your health** and take action to keep fit.
- **Get to know your family better.**
- **Happiness** is more important than money!

This may be rather a mouthful when put together like this, but these brief statements would appear to represent some fundamental truths experienced by these Third Agers who have each had to face the change themselves. The authors are immensely grateful to the participants for taking the trouble to share their thoughts with us in this way.

7

Self-Knowledge: The Basis For Planning Ahead

How well do we really know ourselves? Experience suggests that most of us live more on the surface than we would care to admit, and are carried forward indeterminately on a sea of activities and events which materialise before us. In other words, if we are in a given job or role we tend to carry out the functions required in that position and make the most of what the role affords. But how often do we ask ourselves whether or not we are enjoying the experience, or whether we might perhaps be able to spend our time differently or do something more fulfilling?

The great advantage of a major transition point in our lives is that it gives us just such an opportunity to challenge ourselves. We have the chance to take more control over our lives and to influence the future positively. This is particularly true in the case of someone leaving their main career activity, especially if it involves leaving the employment of a substantial firm or institution, such as public service.

How can we possibly decide what to do next, though, if we have little idea of what we are capable, what really motivates us and what are our deepest aspirations for the future? In our counselling work with Future Perfect we have come across a number of people who find this concept difficult. They tend to tell themselves (somewhat gleefully) that they have reached the departure point from their firm and deserve the reward of leisure, travel and doing nothing that is in the offing.

The fact that they may only be 50 is a bonus, because they will be able to spend more years in this euphoric condition. Yet we know from experience that this is frequently not the outcome for a person with such an attitude; quite the reverse, in fact. He or she is merely mouthing the words formed by an outdated pattern of full-time employment and retirement at 65, with death following shortly after. The reality is that many mature people settle for a mundane, routine existence within very limited boundaries; some even atrophy and are unable to maintain an outgoing social attitude and an active recreational life. So the secret, we suggest, is that we should try to explore our innermost thoughts, the core of our being, if we are to continue to develop our lives and careers through mid-life and beyond.

Anthony de Mello, a mystic and therapist, writes in his book *Awareness* (Fount Paperbacks, 1990) that we should attempt to become much more aware of reality, and that we should aim to strip off the more superficial layers in our thinking, talking and relating to people. A device he recommends for this is to separate the 'I' from the real 'me', and to imagine that the 'I' is looking on (objectively at a distance) at the way the 'me' is behaving. This is a potentially valuable approach when exploring thoughts and actions to arrive at a greater sense of reality and self-understanding.

In this book, however, we are more concerned with the impact that such concepts may have on our future lives and careers, principally from mid-life (40 plus) onwards. The mid-life review process that we have developed in Future Perfect is summarised in Figure 7.1. In order to progress our thinking we have found it helpful to carry out a number of simple exercises to identify different aspects of our motivations, skills and experience. The main purpose is to highlight priority features in our personal lives as a contribution to the life planning process. These exercises, which should be carried out over a period of time, are described under separate headings.

Drawing Up a Life Map

A beneficial initial focus for reviewing one's life pattern are the key family and personal activities and occurrences since early childhood

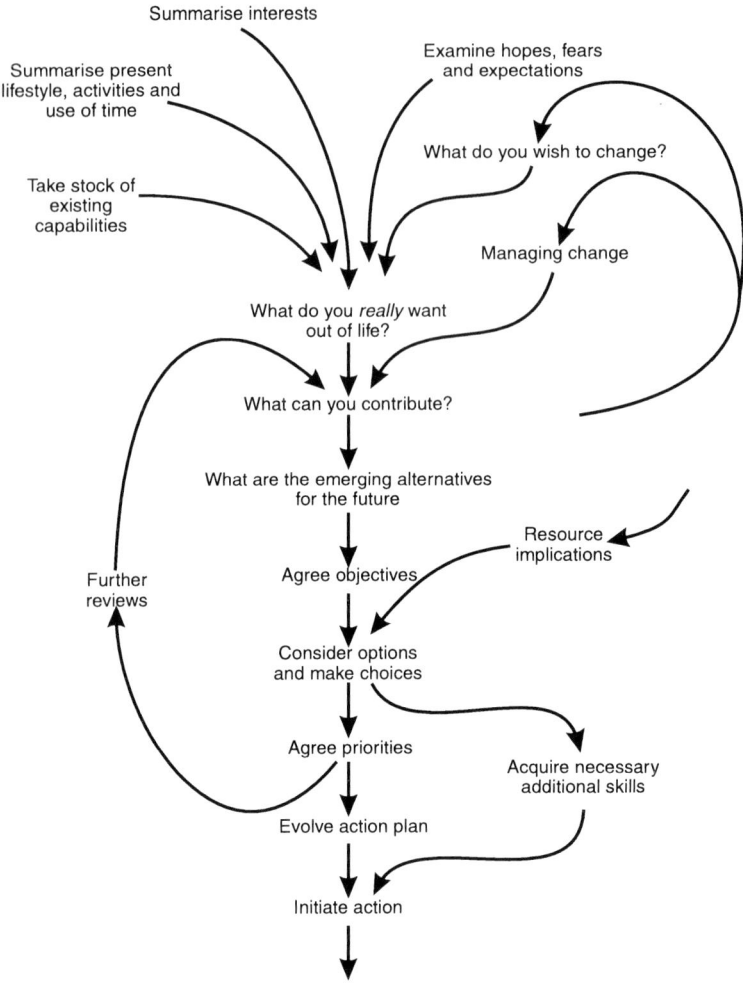

Figure 7.1 Mid-life transition: the review process

up to the present time. If we are planning to gain the highest level of fulfilment from our future lives it stands to reason that we should cast our
minds back on those events and influences which have shaped our lives
so far and satisfied us most. It is possible, through exploration of past
memories and experiences, to highlight some important motivations

and satisfactions. Only through careful reflection can one recall the feelings one had at a particular point in time, e.g. when learning to drive a car and passing a driving test, or owning one's first bicycle or car! You should therefore delve into your memory and draw out those historical events, activities or achievements which have made a significant impact on your life, and your current feelings about them. They will relate to happenings of varying kinds and should include career, personal and family high or low points from childhood onwards.

We don't often give ourselves the time or even the 'permission' to look at ourselves in this way. To lend a framework to your thinking we have prepared a sheet (Table 7.2) upon which you may set out in abbreviated form the main events in your life in the space provided, related to your age at the time. For an illustration of typical features see Table 7.1 below.

Nursery School	Junior School	Secondary School	College	First Job	Met Doris	Married	Father died
0			20				30
Period:							
	Growing Up		Getting a degree	Start of career		Marriage and parenting	

Table 7.1 Section from a life map

We have found that the most effective way of achieving this is to close one's eyes and imagine that you are, for example, actually in your grandmother's house enjoying her cooking. It is frequently experiences that occurred in childhood and earlier life which set a pattern for lifelong interests. A colleague of ours recalls that a key point for her was when she was allowed to help plant out seedlings at a garden centre as a young girl; she has since developed an abiding passion for gardening. One of the authors remembered how much he had enjoyed woodwork from the age of 9, and this memory reawakened an interest in making furniture as a hobby.

Table 7.2 Past events, influences and satisfactions

Satisfactions

Events

Age Group: 0   Childhood/Teenage 20   Young Adulthood   30

Periods

30   Prime Adulthood   40   Mid-Life   50   Maturity

The emphasis in such reflections should, of course, be positive if the object is to highlight past satisfactions which can influence a future lifestyle. Some memories may, however, be painful and it is quite reasonable to write these in as well, because many a fulfilled life has emerged from addressing past sadnesses and helping others in similar situations. Sufficient time should therefore be allowed for adequate periods of reflection. One colleague and his wife carried out this exercise separately from each other, and found it a somewhat overwhelming experience to see how frequently the other partner's name appeared in their life maps when sharing the findings later on!

Once the relevant events have been filled in, think carefully about the various satisfactions involved (or otherwise if significant) and note the particular pleasures or sense of fulfilment that they gave you. You should let your thoughts range freely over your life and write in whatever springs to mind – so why not have a go now!

Current Enjoyments

Having reviewed the past, let's look in some depth at the present. The purpose of this exercise is to highlight particular qualities about yourself based on what you really enjoy doing and how you spend your time. It is likely that you will be more effective at the activities you enjoy doing (and would like to give more time to, perhaps), which may be a pointer to the way in which you should adjust your time, money and efforts in the future.

For example, someone who likes going to and giving parties is likely to be sociable and outgoing, with particular relationship skills which could be developed in all sorts of ways. Someone who gets a huge kick out of sailing may be more independent, with another range of qualities.

So we suggest that you should spend a little time listing what you most enjoy doing in the framework provided below, in which we have included some category headings to help you think this through.

In my **Family Life**:

....
....
....
....
....
....

In my **Work**:

....
....
....
....
....
....

In my **Leisure** (arts, crafts, sport, holidays, etc.):

....
....
....
....
....
....

With my **Friends**:

....
....
....
....
....
....

In other **Pursuits** (community, church, special hobby, etc):

....

....

....

....

....

....

Accomplishments or Satisfactions

In drawing up your life map you will have highlighted a number of instances which will have given you a special satisfaction, and further reflection may yield a few more. Perhaps a suitable trigger might be to look for situations where you have surprised yourself, such as passing an exam you didn't think you had a chance of passing, overcoming a disability, making a piece of furniture, redecorating a room, making a dress, giving a speech, getting a promotion, bringing up a child, and so on. These instances represent very valuable material in helping to identify significant personal qualities that you may have overlooked. If you study these instances carefully they should reveal some important, underlying qualities you possess, addressing life in greater depth than might be readily apparent.

Participants in Future Perfect programmes are asked to identify at least three situations and then examine them in the way indicated in the three examples shown below:

Life satisfaction – example 1
Title: Making a Dress for my Daughter

How did it start?

I was short of money and my daughter badly wanted a dress for a friend's party. I had never been any good at needlework but I thought that I would have a go.

What did you do?

I went to our local department store and looked at patterns labelled 'Easy to Make'. I chose one which seemed to suit her and then bought some fabric (the assistant was very helpful). I borrowed my sister's sewing machine, practised on some old dusters and eventually followed the instructions on the pattern. Though it took two weeks, and a lot of sweating, my daughter was delighted and wore it to the party. The slightly crooked seams didn't seem to matter too much!

What did you most enjoy about the experience?

I never thought I could do it. I did it by myself, it saved a lot of money and gave her pleasure.

What personal qualities did the experience point to?

Resourcefulness, caring, thriftiness, determination, a needlework/craft capability that I didn't believe I possessed.

Life satisfaction – example 2
Title: Taking Part in my School Play

How did it start?

The school was short of volunteers and our English teacher asked me to play the part of the Wall in 'A Midsummer Night's Dream'.

What did you do?

I had never acted before and was very apprehensive, but we had plenty of rehearsals and I was able to learn my lines. It was strange to dress up as a wall and it was a nerve-racking experience. When it happened, though, everyone in the audience started laughing and the act went off without any problems.

What did you most enjoy about the experience?

Discovering that I could do something quite well that I had never done before or even contemplated doing. I was surprised how much I enjoyed being in front of an audience.

What personal qualities did the experience point to?

Courage, persistence, speaking and performing skills, team player.

Life satisfaction – example 3
Title: Building a Hovercraft

How did it start?

A visiting teacher at school was a hovercraft enthusiast and I was attracted to building one.

What did you do?

My hobby was making things and I enrolled for extra workshop periods at school. I made furniture and equipment out of wood and various kinds of metal. This external teacher was a keen racer of hovercrafts and once brought his machine to the workshop. I became interested and, with his encouragement, built a hovercraft from working drawings which he gave me. It took about six months and was a great success; I was given the workshop prize and the hovercraft was shown in action on Sports Day.

What did you most enjoy about the experience?

I like making things and this was particularly satisfying because it was the first ever hovercraft to be built at the school. I enjoyed the recognition that this gave me, and the prize that went with it.

What personal qualities did the experience point to?

Enterprise, innovation, creativity, mechanical/electrical capability, determination, commitment, planning and organising strengths.

Now take at least three occurrences from your own life and describe the process you went through by filling in the following frameworks:

Life satisfaction – your example 1

Title: ....

How did it start?: ....

....

....

....

....

....

What did you do?: ....

....

....

....

....

....

What did you most enjoy about the experience?: ....

....

....

....

What personal qualities did the experience point to?:

....

....

....

....

....

Life satisfaction – your example 2

Title: ....

How did it start?: ....

....

....

....

....

....

What did you do?: ....

....

....

....

....

....

What did you most enjoy about the experience?: ....

....

....

....

....

....

What personal qualities did the experience point to?:

....

....

....

....

....

Life satisfaction – your example 3

Title: ....

How did it start?: ....
....
....
....
....
....

What did you do?: ....
....
....
....
....
....

What did you most enjoy about the experience?: ....
....
....
....
....
....

What personal qualities did the experience point to?:
....
....
....
....
....

Skills

We undoubtedly possess more skills than we are prepared to acknowledge, as indicated by the previous exercise. It is sometimes helpful to make a check against a simple skills list to ensure that we haven't missed out anything vital when compiling an inventory of strengths, skills, qualities and satisfactions. We suggest that you put a tick or a cross against the check list in the first instance, and then select the top 10 skill definitions that you rate most highly. Have a go – you might surprise yourself!

Skills checklist

What are you good at doing?

Relating to people as individuals

- **Caring**, supporting, consoling, helping
- **Nursing** sick people
- **Listening**
- **Talking**
- **Visiting** lonely or distressed people
- **Writing** letters
- **Tutoring**, mentoring
- **Persuading**, selling ideas, or products/services
- **Networking**, facilitating link-ups
- **Appraising** people.

Relating to people in groups

- **Speaking** in public, or to a group
- **Facilitating** group interaction, discussion
- **Managing** a project, business or home activity
- **Writing** a book, play or articles
- **Leading** or hosting an activity or initiative
- **Entertaining**, performing, acting, joking or artistic roles
- **Meeting targets**, getting things done
- **Sport**, playing a game or recreational activity
- **Training** or teaching

- **Peacemaking**, helping to resolve conflicts
- **Parenting** and all that involves.

Individual activities involving information and creative ideas

- **Manipulating data**, searching, researching and analysing
- **Computing** or word processing
- **Innovating**, creating new concepts
- **Accounting**, number crunching
- **Administering**, organising, planning
- **Problem-solving**, providing solutions
- **Drawing**, painting or designing
- **Photographing**, making videos
- **Reading**, fantasising or philosophising
- **Spiritual reflection**, contemplation, praying
- **Music**, playing an instrument, singing
- **Physical exercise**, jogging, working out in the gym, yoga, dancing.

Working with materials, machines, or natural objects

- **Handicrafts**, working with wood, metal, stone, cloth, etc.
- **Cooking**, preparing meals
- **Machinery operation**, restoration or repair
- **Housework**, washing, keeping a home clean and tidy
- **Home improvement**, DIY, redecorating, building, working with tools
- **Driving** and looking after a vehicle
- **Caring for animals**, feeding and looking after them
- **Gardening**, growing and nurturing plants, trees, etc.

Now make sure you highlight the top 10 skill areas that you have identified.

Which of the following *most* describe me? Am I a....

Thinking Person	**Person of Integrity**	**Strong Character**	**Change Agent**
Astute	Loyal	Determined	Innovative
Analytical	Honest	Powerful	Imaginative
Perceptive	Committed	Persistent	Creative
Inquisitive	Reliable	Tenacious	Visionary
Thoughtful	Faithful	Dominant	Risk-taking
Intellectual	Dedicated	Focused	Designing
Intelligent	Trusting	Decisive	Idealistic
Cautious	Principled	Forceful	Enterprising
	Conscientious	Autocratic	Restless
	Stable	Assertive	Open-minded

Motivator	**Helper**	**Relator**	**Doer**
Positive	Empathic	Sociable	Achieving
Enthusiastic	Caring	Amenable	Results-oriented
Encouraging	Sympathique	Flexible	Driving
Persuasive	Sharing	Humorous	Ambitious
Leading	Enabling	Friendly	Competitive
Constructive	Listening	Responsive	Busy
Optimistic	Co-operative	Adaptable	Pragmatic
Inspirational	Supportive	Team-working	Quick to act
	Sensitive		Versatile
	Giving		Competing

Co-ordinator	**Loner**	**Self-Publicist**	**Conciliator**
Planning	Self-confident	Performing	Mediating
Organising	Independent	Recognised	Negotiating
Delegating	Resourceful	Acting	Fair
Structured	Introvert	Extrovert	Following
Methodical	Solitary	Presentable	Accepting
Objective	Reflecting	Exhibitionist	Understanding
Arranging		Prominent	

Table 7.3 Personal characteristics

Personal Characteristics

We have developed an informal categorisation of types of people that we have observed in the course of our work. This is a straightforward, unsophisticated attempt to help people identify the sort of person they actually are, as compared with others. Some may consider that they can relate to all the characteristics shown in Table 7.3, but most of us would acknowledge that some descriptions apply much more to us than to others. We therefore suggest that you should tick the main headings you consider apply to you (probably five or six) as a first step. Then circle the actual subsidiary words that you feel describe you most accurately (no more than ten!).

Strengths, Skills, Qualities Inventory

You now have a range of personal attributes that you can list. We suggest that you set all these out below to summarise the situation, drawing upon the findings of each of the exercises you have carried out.

Current enjoyments:
I particularly enjoy: ....
....
....
....

Accomplishments/Satisfactions:
My past experience shows that I have the following personal qualities:
....
....
....

Skills:
My top 10 skills I have identified as being: ....
....
....
....

Personal characteristics:

I would describe myself as being: ....

....

....

....

So you now have a valuable inventory of personal qualities upon which you can build a life and career plan for the next five to 10 years.

Aim In Life

Many of us take life as it comes, and do not acknowledge any sense of direction from external or internal causes. One lady who participated in this particular session claimed that she had never really taken any major life decisions herself, yet she was married to a bank manager, had a beautiful daughter, and lived in a house in a desirable area. She felt that she had drifted into all of this and expected that the rest of her life would continue to unfold in a similar way.

There are others, too, who might claim that the organisation they worked for gave them their main purpose in life, that their job was really all that mattered to them; provided they worked hard and climbed up the promotion ladder, all would be well.

Life is not like that in reality, as most of us appreciate. Possibly we may have relied too much in the past on others making decisions for us – our parents, our partner, our boss, our colleagues, the state – but this is unlikely to be the case mid-life and beyond, however. Lifetime employment with one or more organisations has disappeared for most, and everyone at any age in any job is vulnerable to the relatively swift implications of adverse economic and commercial conditions. As they say at Marks and Spencer: 'Security of employment is not about being employed, but about being *employable.*' So it is difficult for people who have worked loyally for organisations for numbers of years to come to terms with a career transition, whether this occurs at 30, 40, 50 or 60. Any impending transition, however, provides a valuable opportunity for challenging ourselves and asking, 'What is my genuine aim in life from now on for the foreseeable future?'

Most of us will have an unspoken aim fairly deep inside us which we have never articulated. Yet we are all different and can have very varied aspirations lying under the surface. In our counselling work we have found that it is immensely valuable for this aim to be discovered, articulated and nurtured if we are to identify our preferred future directions and tap the deeper motivations that exist within us. This may seem a somewhat esoteric concept, but people's lives have been significantly improved through a better understanding of what they care about.

We recommend that you devote quite a bit of time to reflection on what you consider to be your aim in life. A client of one of the authors spent several hours in her garden mulling this over and came up with a remarkable output, which touched her deeply. You can either settle for an instant, superficial version therefore, or be prepared to challenge yourself over a longer period of time that you can identify with closely and which is unique to you. It is not about fulfilling duty roles, of keeping up appearances, of pleasing your husband, wife, parents or children – it's about *your* personal aim in life. None of us know when we are going to die, but there might not be too much time left!

Charles Handy, amongst others, asks his students to write their obituary to highlight what they want out of life, what you would like said about you when you die. You are free to do this if you wish, but we suggest that you start the process by considering your aim in each of the following areas:

My aim in life is to:

In my family: ....

....

....

....

In my work ....

....

....

....

With my money: ....

....

....

....

With my friends: ....

....

....

....

In my spiritual life:...

....

....

....

For the community:...

....

....

....

For myself and my leisure: ....

....

....

....

You should now have the priority elements for constructing a suitably comprehensive summary statement, which you will then be able to remember as a visible objective for your life planning and subsequent action. Here are three examples from other people:

- 'To fulfil my gifts and opportunities, working to my strengths and improving my weaknesses, broadly in the service of others and in bringing up a caring next generation.'

- 'To become financially independent, to maintain an active business life until my faculties start to fail, and to establish closer relationships with people I meet in the course of work and leisure.'

- 'To be fulfilled as a person through giving and receiving love, particularly within the family, and pursuing a variety of business, people and spiritual interests.'

Try to pull together the various parts of your detailed aims and include them in a draft statement below – don't worry if you don't get it right first time.

Write out your final statement opposite, and if you are happy with it copy it on a yellow sticker and put it near your desk, bed, kitchen or wherever you will often notice it to remind you of your priority aims.

....
....
....
....
....
....

If you get stuck, here are some artificially constructed examples for different types of people which may stimulate you to include certain features that had not occurred to you.

Aim in life - examples

The Ambitious Type

'My aim in life is to develop my career to the full, using every opportunity to advance my position and achieve high levels of recognition and reward in the future.'

The Family Person

'My aim in life is to achieve a successful career so that I am able to provide adequate support to my family, both emotionally and financially, in the coming years.'

The Planner

'My aim in life is to continue working in my main career as long as is practically possible and to plan for realising financial independence and a stimulating portfolio of activities in my Third Age.'

The Professional

'My aim in life is to capitalize on my specialist, professional skills and experience broadly in the service of others and to provide an adequate income for me and my family.'

The Breadwinner

'My aim in life is to earn enough money to pay off the mortgage and educate my son and daughter by the time I am 55, so that I can retire early and be financially independent.'

The Idealist

'My aim in life is to change direction and do something different in order to maintain a high level of personal interest and achieve a varied and fulfilling career.'

The Entrepreneur

'My aim in life is to use my specialist skills in a new, self-employed capacity and to achieve greater freedom by offering my services to purchasing units in an imaginative way.'

The Reformer

'My aim in life is to become a better person by being less selfish and concentrating more on helping others, including family, friends and the community at large.'

The Academic

'My aim in life is to realise a long-held ambition to publish a book which will provide a valuable contribution in my specialist area and will bring me significant personal recognition among colleagues and others of importance in a wider field.'

The Targeted Achiever

'My aim in life is to get a better job based on my extensive range of skills and experience so that I can live in the style to which I would like to become accustomed (posher house, bigger car, glamorous holidays).'

8

Examining Specific Career And Life Opportunities

What Really Is Available To Me At This Stage In My Life?

You have set out, after considerable thought, your declared priorities in your 'aim in life' statement. No doubt this has been done with a certain amount of trepidation, because it may include a whole range of activities that are either entirely new or have not been experienced for many years. Shall I be able to cope with the demands of this strange new role? Shall I be able to learn the new techniques that are necessary? Will I fit into the unknown culture in a new environment? Am I being too ambitious? Or not ambitious enough? These are the sort of questions that flood into one's mind at this critical juncture.

Some people who have made a major transition earlier in their career, such as army officers or expatriates returning from overseas, will already have experienced this situation and will find the feelings to be similar. Most of us, however, will have spent 20 years or more in our main career and will be unfamiliar with the need to make such critical life and career decisions – usually within a relatively short period of time, because we tend to deny the fact that we have to move on and put our thoughts on hold.

The authors know a personnel director who confessed that a meeting to discuss Future Perfect's role had brought home to him for the first time that he would actually be retiring in a year's time! He then had to admit to himself that he had not been facing up to the need to decide what he was going to do with the rest of his life – it was a great shock.

As we have indicated earlier, the opportunities for taking up different and fulfilling types of work or recreational activity in the Third Age are almost limitless. The key to whether or not they exist for you will depend on what you have declared as being your aim in life – or, if it doesn't sound too esoteric, what is simmering in the depths of your being. This is often the time of life when some buried desire can emerge very strongly, despite being hidden for so long, with the owner being completely unaware of the potential for fulfilment underneath the surface.

Our recent research revealed one person, a senior professional partner in a notable firm, who confessed that his life and career had only really taken off after he had 'retired' in his fifties! The interesting feature is that virtually no one, as they step towards the brink of the Third Age, can determine whether what they hope to do will be successful or indeed whether it might turn out to be quite different from what they had expected. The research indicates that surprises lie ahead for almost everyone – but they are usually positive features rather than disappointments.

Before considering different life and career options that might be of appeal, and making relevant choices, we suggest that much more attention should be given to pondering just what might be available and then mulling it over in one's mind at some length. One of our respondents in the research, quoted earlier in this book, put it succinctly like this:

'Don't rush. Give yourself time to think why you are changing. Get in touch with what you feel strongly about. Talk to people and let the ideas marinate. Experiment; it's OK to change your mind. You don't have to justify what you are doing to anyone but yourself. Share your hopes and fears with your partner as honestly as possible. Go for it and good luck.'

We believe this to be extremely good advice. The biggest danger at this critical stage in life, is that you could pursue somewhat blindly occupations and activities with which you are already familiar, and perhaps miss out on other opportunities waiting round the corner that might be more fulfilling. There is nothing wrong with carrying on working in a field in which you are well established, particularly if earning significant sums of money is important to you, but a new slant or different approach could provide a fresh impetus to a life and career.

To give two specific examples, both the authors used to be full-time management consultants with well-known consultancy firms. One, Barry, now runs his own organisation called Maresfield Curnow, which concentrates on 'training, coaching and mentoring by management consultants for management consultants' – it is still very much in the management consulting field, but is quite different from Barry's former existence and capitalises on his particular strengths. The other author, John, became involved with Future Perfect which specialises in 'consultancy and counselling for people and organisations in transition' and Science Cities, an economic development and business generation company with a reputation for technoparks (establishing and creating new businesses) – both related to people and business consultancy, but from a very different perspective from John's former role.

The fundamental point about these two examples is that each of us has changed our jobs very considerably and become involved with new ventures – the new careers are a far cry from conventional management consultancy as practised by the larger firms, but have been built on our skills, experience and personal aspirations. In addition, we have both developed other interests and activities beyond those mentioned and operate on Charles Handy's 'portfolio' basis, having benefited from knowing him personally. We can both say without equivocation that we would have been less enthused and less fulfilled if we had adopted the traditional route of working as a 'sole practitioner' consultant, though many of our colleagues have done just this and claim to find it satisfying.

So, it is for this reason, based on our personal experience, that we urge you to spend quite some time mulling over the wide range of possibilities that exist for you to consider as your special means of achieving your stated aim in life. To help you with this task we are setting out below an overview of the main areas that present appropriate opportunities, and we then describe each 'family' of activities in further detail later on.

Overview of Third Age Life and Career Opportunities

1. Operating independently as a self-employed contractor

- using relevant skills and experience
- setting up and operating from a 'home office'
- becoming self-employed
- using personal networks or an agency to get work.

2. Becoming a specialist consultant, alone or with others

- taking advantage of specialist skills and experience
- creating, in effect, a new consultancy business
- developing defined products to meet a specific market need
- building and updating a relevant business plan
- launching and operating successfully.

3. Fulfilling the role of a non-executive director>

- normally based on previous Board experience
- legally responsible role
- personal and business links a significant factor
- more demanding than generally perceived.

4. Starting up a new manufacturing or service business with others

- an ideal chance to 'run one's own show'
- identifying and testing out appropriate business ideas
- examining the scope for licence or joint venture
- choosing the right people as your core team
- researching the market for the chosen product range
- developing an acceptable business plan
- raising appropriate finance, based on the plan
- launching and operating the new business.

5. Working for the community or for a charity

- examining local and national scope for community work
- identifying personal interests and finding matching organisations
- giving something back, yet finding it more rewarding than you ever expected
- starting up new local branch of national charity
- being trained and operating as a volunteer in a chosen charity
- taking up a role as a Justice of the Peace, School Governor, etc.

6. Learning new skills or enhancing knowledge in a chosen field

- exploring personal aspirations and potential areas of interest
- researching the scope for learning opportunities
- selecting possible course options at a suitable college or university
- choosing preferred programme after testing it out
- committing your time, learning energetically and getting your qualification.

7. Becoming a teacher, counsellor, adviser or mentor

- using personal qualities to help others
- developing the necessary skills or gaining a new qualification
- focusing on personal interaction, either in a group or on a one-to-one basis
- determining mode of operation – from 'gift work' through to business activity.

8. Developing hobbies

- identifying which hobby to devote more time and effort to
- developing a plan to increase involvement in the chosen activity
- considering participation in a relevant holiday or other skill-based initiative
- achieving your personal goals in the identified field.

9. Sport, travel or leisure

- the opportunity to visit and do all those things you wanted to do but had no time
- planning new initiatives and adventures

- starting something completely different, e.g. mountain-biking, scuba diving
- promoting a healthy lifestyle
- enjoying more concerts, plays, tournaments, games, holidays than ever before!

10. Do something outrageous

Such as (all genuine examples):

- sail the Atlantic, or anywhere, for a year or so
- buy a Dutch barge in France, do it up, and live in it for much of the year
- sell your house and buy a mansion in the country
- throw up your job and become a woodwork (furniture) apprentice for two years
- cycle from Prague to Venice
- challenge your partner and yourself to be outrageous!

Explorations into Specific Life and Career Opportunities

Introduction

We are now going to explore each of the opportunities highlighted earlier in greater depth. Before doing so, however, it would seem appropriate to discuss the one obvious opportunity when leaving your main career that we haven't yet referred to – getting another employed job! We deliberately haven't yet mentioned this as an option because we find that this rather tempting, superficially easy quest will normally result in a great deal of frustration and depression for a mature person, and in fact will prevent you from addressing the fundamental issue of what you realistically want to do with the rest of your life. Any new, employed job would be likely to be relatively short-term unless, of course, it were actually a continuation of your main career (and could not really be considered to be a Third Age activity). This route should certainly be explored, however, particularly if a continuing income were a high priority.

It would be inappropriate for us to add to the vast amount of material written about the steps that need to be taken to secure a new, employed post. This represents a standard process used by personnel specialists and outplacement consultants alike, which can achieve some remarkable results for people in mid-career. It is much less easy for someone aged 45 plus, though, because, whatever we may be asked to believe, ageism is a key factor in recruitment when there is an oversupply of labour. We have observed this feature time and time again, and it is something that you cannot afford to ignore. We therefore suggest that the following aspects should be considered if you wish to explore this route:

- **Analyse where your strengths and weaknesses lie** regarding potential employment. Be realistic and define clear boundaries as to what may be possible in terms of job specification, earnings level, industry sector, location, travel and other costs incurred. It is no good saying that you would be prepared to take anything – it is unconvincing to a prospective employer and just doesn't work in practice. You need to have thought things through exceptionally well in order to present a positive picture, based on your evident skills and experience, to stand any chance of being considered for a given post. This should be supported by a well-presented personal profile or CV, on which you should take advice if you haven't prepared one recently – this is your main selling document.

- **Test out the market** by writing in response to a few selected advertisements in the fields you have chosen. The purpose of this activity is not so much to get the job (though that would be a welcome bonus!) but to assess the impact and validity of your approach, preferably as result of obtaining one or two interviews. These interviews can be valuable learning experiences, and it is possible to assess the chances of getting a similar job if you are able to be objective – most people tend to know the positive and negative aspects of an interview if they are honest with themselves.

- **Develop a positive plan** to approach certain organisations you would like to work for – to fit in with your defined requirements and the experience gained during your initial search. At this stage you should take advantage of your personal network of contacts and, by one means or another, find ways of using 'warm' leads to approach those firms set out in your plan. Research has shown that you are more likely to get another job through this planned, proactive approach than through responding endlessly to adverts, which can be a dreadful waste of time and induce bouts of depression. Provided you have targeted this activity effectively, and have been realistic about your potential, you stand a good chance of eventually bringing home the bacon.

The main point we are trying to make is that, depending on your age, the priority should be to work out what is going to satisfy you not only for the immediate future but for the years ahead as you pass 50, 60 and 70! It may be appropriate to get another corporate job for a limited number of years, but what is going to happen after that? Leaving your main career presents you with the ideal opportunity for a reappraisal and change of direction that will endure for many years to come. This is the reason why we have concentrated on different non-corporate opportunities, and the following pages attempt to explore each of these categories in further detail.

1. Operating Independently as a Self-Employed Contractor

The most natural path for someone leaving their main career is to offer themselves as a freelance operator, either directly with various firms or via an employment agency such as those existing for secretaries, engineers, nurses and countless other professions. It requires a totally different approach to that of an employee, however, which is where many fall down on implementing this concept.

The main difference is that it becomes necessary to sell yourself and your capability on an ongoing basis – at the end of the day if you are successful you will be employed only on a short-term contract (maximum of three months likely) and will need to remind your purchaser regularly how very valuable you are to the continued progress of the organisation. The tips we would offer in this situation to ensure optimum effectiveness are as follows:

- **Define your market** in which your skills and experience will be pre-eminent. This is most likely to be related to your previous core activities, but needs careful definition in the light of the potential you see for your personal capability. A particular emphasis may need to be given to a past activity for which there is currently more demand than for something carried out more recently.

- **Prepare your personal profile**, which will, in effect, be your sales brochure. This may seem unnecessary or objectionable at first, but we would assure you that time spent on preparing and producing a sound and imaginative profile document will be well worthwhile. This, apart from personal recommendations, will be all that a prospective purchaser will have to go on initially and is consequently disproportionately important.

- **Approach your market,** having first determined your plan of attack. You may well have decided to use an appropriate agency if there is one that suits your particular capability, and that is a relatively straightforward process. In this case, though, you are depending on the agency to do your selling for you, and they will take a share of your earnings for so doing. As long as you are happy with this way of working that is fine; it certainly suits a great many people who don't want to be bothered with the sales and admin involved in operating independently. If, however, you choose to strike out on your own we suggest that you should first consider *previous employers* who know you well and secondly *suppliers* and *customers* with whom you have had close contact. There is a distinct advantage for a purchaser to employ someone who already has specialist, local knowledge unique to an organisation, and you should place great emphasis on that capability. It is very expensive to train people from scratch and the learning process in adapting to a firm's particular culture can have a very adverse effect on productivity until the person concerned becomes entirely familiar with the new ways of working. So you could be a gift to that organisation – there are no training costs, no continuing employment obligations, no fixed hours, no holiday costs. It is hardly surprising that there has been a significant increase in part-time working for former employees or equivalent mature staff in recent years. This is very often ideal for the Third Ager who wants to build a varied portfolio of activities, so that he or she is able to complement this activity with other paid or non-paid activities.

The implications regarding income tax and National Insurance are relatively straightforward. You should notify your tax office of your change in circumstances, and they will make an assessment concerning the amount of income tax and National Insurance contribution you should pay – delayed by several months, which is one of the benefits of being self-employed (though it requires a relevant financial discipline to ensure that the money will be available by the twice-yearly due dates!). It would probably be helpful to receive advice, preferably from a qualified accountant, when completing your first income tax return as a self-employed person. Provided one maintains meticulous records, therefore, there should be few problems in making the change from an employed to a self-employed method of working.

An essential requirement, in the authors' view, for almost any Third Age activity is to set up a 'home office'. The reasons for this are varied, some not at first obvious, but the main one is that you become no longer dependent on anyone else for organising your business life. When operating a portfolio career it is virtually impossible to delegate office tasks to the firms or people with whom you are working on an occasional basis. We speak from direct experience in emphasising that, when the chips are down, you have to be able to, for example, type, print and bind a high-quality report for a given deadline *entirely by yourself* if you are to stand a chance of being successful.

The other reasons for organising yourself to be self-sufficient office-wise are that it is satisfying to be able to cope with something you were convinced was beyond you, and it is actually fun to be able to keep up with and take advantage of developments in technology! It is also of considerable benefit to have your office facilities available for any charitable or leisure activities with which you or your family are involved. Many are the brochures that one of the authors has produced as a result of having this facility, and he and his family have been wondering how they ever existed beforehand without a photocopier on site!

The other author has gone even further and is a regular user of the Internet – one might almost say that he has made the transition to being computer-literate! This really is an exciting opportunity, though, and it is absolute rubbish to say that mature men and women are unable to grasp new technology and new ways of doing things; when the potential benefits are realised we can assure you that a home office soon becomes highly operational.

Ben Cannon, chief executive of Alexander Workwear, the executive clothing firm, says that in future, consultants who are not computer-literate will not work or eat! It is a basic survival and life skill for a small business.

On the technology front, we have found a summary produced by the Institute of Management Consultants for their members in the form of an Electronic Communications Briefing Note to be a helpful guide in appreciating just what *communications services* are actually available. The Institute has kindly allowed us to reproduce the following extract, relating to the possible options that you can take up via your personal computer:

- **Electronic mail:** Electronic mail, using personal computers, offers the unique facility of freedom from the need to make contacts at a particular time convenient to both parties, and allows messages to be exchanged directly by individuals or small groups. The communication channel depends critically on the third party, the 'service provider', on whose computer system all communications are stored. In such services, messages are unrestricted in length but they cannot be used for word processing or spreadsheet files in their original form.

- **Sending and receiving files:** Sometimes files must be transferred in their full detail, e.g. as a WORD 6 file to be used in WORD 6 at the receiving end without having to be retranslated. Service providers generally allow this to take place easily within their own service, using an automatic encoding procedure which translates the binary file into a form using only the basic text character set.

- **Bulletin boards:** This is a facility giving wide access to information posted by individuals to the electronic equivalent of a notice board. It provides a means of allowing those with common interests or problems to exchange views or share experiences. It is widely used by distributors of computer programs and packages to update their products. Bulletin board services have particular features which depend on the software used by the service provider.

- **Conferences:** Certain services allow private, restricted membership conferences to be set up by individual members, led and moderated by one of their number. It should be noted that such conferences can be convened only when all members use a service provider with this service available.

- **Databases:** Some service providers are primarily in the business of providing information. Thus one can find published company information, travel timetables and reservation services, legal information and much other useful information available on demand.

- **The Internet:** The technical problems having been overcome, the process of linking different service providers to offer a continuous channel of communication is now an established fact. Most now provide full Internet addressing which offers world-wide communications. Furthermore, it is also possible to have direct access to the World Wide Web by using the Internet, which opens up a very extensive range of information services to the ordinary user. There are still some drawbacks in using the World Wide Web for business purposes, however, because the traffic on the 'Information Superhighway' frequently gets jammed, reducing speeds to a crawl, but these problems are being overcome and the Net is becoming a widely used channel for worldwide communication for business.

With regard to **hardware and software requirements** the following comments are made:

- The personal computers currently in use for WINDOWS-based word processing are more than equal to the task of handling communications. The only additional hardware needed is a modem to enable the computer to use an ordinary telephone line. It can be quite difficult to develop satisfactory initialisation procedures for some modems if they have not already been prepared. It is essential to check that the software needed for a particular modem is available; the service provider should advise on this.

- Finding basic communications software normally presents no problem, provided that an appropriate modem has been installed. Such basic software, when properly set up, dials the number and makes the connection to the service. The keyboard has then to be used 'on-line' to generate the appropriate commands to operate the service.

- A much better arrangement is to use the software, which allows almost all the keyboard work to be done locally, before connecting to the service. With this arrangement the telephone connection can proceed uninterrupted at a speed of several thousand characters a second, which saves both line and service charges.

The above represents only the briefest summary of the implications and potential opportunities available in the electronic communications front, taking advantage of your personal computer. Many will not wish to extend beyond fairly basic word processing, but we felt that a suitable commentary should be inserted to help you to determine just what you wish to install in your new home office.

We now put forward a few tips about the necessary steps to be taken in setting up a home office, based on our experience. We suggest that the following should act as a check list if you are considering doing this from scratch:

- Decide which room to use, since there are quite a few implications regarding this choice. Ideally the room should be slightly apart from the general run of the house, such as a top-floor room or room over a garage, but this is not always possible. If there is a couple who both require office facilities to some degree we strongly recommend that there should be two separate offices if at all possible – it is actually the personal space for creativity and development that you will be constructing. The mechanics are a secondary consideration in our view, and one of the main benefits of a home office should be that you have many fewer interruptions than you had been used to in your main career! A quiet, independent environment is therefore beneficial for reflective consideration of issues and priorities when you are away from working with clients or carrying out routine tasks.

The room chosen should also be large enough to accommodate a desk, a large table (for collating and binding reports), filing cabinets, bookcase(s), photocopier, personal computer with printer and fax as a minimum. A reasonable size would be 10 ft by 12 ft, we suggest, but plenty of space is helpful as there are always more documents and files on the go than you might ever imagine! For this reason we believe that the designated room should be used solely as a study or office, and that a dual-purpose living/office room should not be considered.

• Decide what equipment will be needed before you rush into buying something you might later regret. We listed above the various articles that you are likely to require as a minimum, and much of it is straightforward. One opportunity you should seize however, before it is too late is to obtain cast-off furniture and equipment from your current firm before you leave. Most firms reject items of value when there is a major refurbishment and are normally prepared to let things go at a nominal value to employees who can make a good case for taking them over. We have known many instances where such assistance has been invaluable and formed the basis for setting up a really effective new operation.

It is naturally the high-tech equipment that is the problem, because this is likely to be a totally new field for the aspiring Third Ager. The technology involved is changing all the while, and it is therefore essential to take the advice of someone who knows more than you do, preferably a computer specialist. A suitable photocopier, however, is not difficult to choose – a catalogue from a office supplies firm like Ryman or Viking may be sufficient information for making the choice.

Your personal computer configuration may be much more difficult to determine because of the wide variety of equipment available. It is now possible to buy a unit that will comprise a sophisticated desk-top publishing and video-editing facility, a CD Rom capability, combined with an international fax and electronic mail facility. There is also the option to purchase a lap-top computer; these are now extremely powerful and capable of almost anything that you might require from a desk-top version. In addition there are the electronic communication facilities available that were referred to above. So you certainly will need advice from someone who knows what they are talking about in order to establish a modern home office that is both advanced technologically and is user-friendly.

- **Become operational**, and that, apart from the mechanics of refurbishment and physical installation, means understanding what all the new equipment is capable of. Though it is possible to muddle through with reference and self-help books there is a sound case for going on relevant training courses for both development of keyboard skills and operation of word processing equipment. If, however, your self-taught two-finger approach enables you to type as fast as you think, you could get by without a training course – it all depends on the level of competence you feel to be acceptable for what you want to achieve. Most software packages have appropriate manuals available in leading bookshops, and these provide the fall-back support you may need from time to time. You should, we suggest, look upon this whole activity as an exciting adventure – a mature version of setting up a model railway!

As a self-employed contractor you will, in fact, be operating a one-person business. This may consist principally of being employed as a sub-contractor, either directly by the client firms themselves or through an agency. You might, however, wish to consider other avenues whilst doing this; there are likely to be many unsolicited opportunities coming your way if you are in the market for a new business initiative. Some will be false or scandalous, such as a recent suggestion to launch a chain mail-type operation and net £50,000 in a very short space of time. Others, though, may be of interest and one recent example has considerable appeal: 'Make a Future-Proof Income with Desk-Top Publishing'. The accompanying blurb starts off 'Yes, the complete Business Start-Up package is all you need to start your own business in Desk-Top Publishing. This is a very lucrative and rewarding industry' – and, not mentioned, quite competitive also! It should, however, be a very attractive proposition to someone who is artistically-minded and who would like to enter a new business with minimal risk; the cost of the package is £220 (anyone interested should phone 0956 701034).

There are also journals which specialise in publicising potential business initiatives, such as the **Business Opportunities Digest**, 28 Charles Square, London N1 6HT. These are mainly one-person activities, and if that is what you are looking for it may be worth pursuing. A similar venture has been mounted by another organisation called **Business Head Start**, 13 Conway Avenue, Carlton, Nottingham NG4 2PY (01602 615017). They publish a considerable number of successful case histories. There is another journal called **Home-Run**, which is specially for 'all who want to work effectively from home'. The publisher is Active Information, 79 Black Lion Lane, London W6 9BG (0181 846 9244).

Another opportunity which we have known to be very successful for some Future Perfect participants is **teaching English as a foreign language**. There is a comprehensive reference book for this activity called the **EFL Guide**, obtainable from EFL Gazette, 10 Wright's Lane, London W8 6TA (0171 937 6506). Another organisation, **Intuition Languages**, 109 Shepperton Road, London N1 3DF (0171 359 7794) specialises in providing overseas students (usually mature) with the opportunity to learn the English language and culture. This is achieved by the student living as a paying guest in the home of the tutor, which allows a great deal of flexibility in terms of formal lesson times and the informal contact with friends and family enhances the learning process considerably. The remuneration for the tutor under these conditions is also attractive, and it therefore presents an ideal opportunity for a former teacher with young children to get back into teaching without too much disruption to the family. We highly recommend this venture.

You may consider the above too demanding to become involved with, but how about offering yourself as a **'Homesitter'**? Homesitters Ltd, Buckland Wharf, Buckland, Aylesbury, HP22 5LQ (01296 630730) employs people of retirement age (they are looking for people aged 40 to 68) to live in other people's homes and care for their pets and possessions while the owners are away. With the increases in crime that we are experiencing you can imagine that there is a strong demand for this service. The average assignment lasts for 10 to 14 days and normally takes place within 80 miles of the Sitter's home. Food, travel expenses and a weekly remuneration make this an attractive proposition for people who enjoy experiencing different home environments.

There are also, of course, franchising opportunities which are aimed directly at the self-employed contractor. We are slightly cautious about such an opportunity because we have seen so many individuals start with great enthusiasm, which then gradually peters out for one reason or another (the selling of water purifiers being a typical instance). Some examples that have come across our desk include a **Skill and Aptitude Testing** opportunity, for which regional franchises were being offered, a **Beverage (coffee and juice) Service**, based on a unique Swedish system, and a **Recruitment Business** support service which would enable you to run your own operation as part of a network of franchised recruitment businesses. Our advice would be to check out the market potential very carefully, and to examine critically (and seek evidence of) the competitive edge of the product or service involved.

Franchising has, however, grown considerably in recent years, and if you want to start up a small business it does have the twin advantages of both minimising the risk and allowing you to become operational within a relatively short space of time. There is a self-regulatory body, the **British Franchise Association**, which acts as a watchdog for franchising. Each year they sponsor the British Franchise Exhibition in conjunction with the CBI, and it is supported by a number of commercial banks and the Department of Trade and

Industry. In 1996 it was held at Wembley, and the big attraction at this exhibition (at which the number of exhibitors had more than doubled compared with the year before) was the diversity of business opportunities demonstrated. It is possible to pay only £10,000 to £15,000 to start a franchise run from home, or £50,000 to £100,000 for a restaurant or retail business, with a facility to borrow a significant proportion of the start-up costs and initial working capital from the banks if necessary. To give you more of an idea of the range of opportunities available, examples at the 1996 exhibition included the following:

- discount voucher scheme to promote local shops and tradespeople
- specialist fabric and material retailing
- Irish sandwich bars, and an American delicatessen
- French bistro-style restaurant (already grown to 92 units)
- retail opportunities such as petrol stations, science fiction and pawnbroking!

2. Becoming a Specialist Consultant, Alone or With Others

We see this as being distinctly different from operating as a self-employed contractor or independent agent, who, in essence, is offering a capability for hire to carry out a given task within an organisation. That task is supervised by someone within the organisation, and the contractor is normally remunerated on an hourly or daily basis related to the agreed amount of time taken up. The contractor is thus employed to carry out a job of work by an organisation, and the responsibility for its success or failure rests solely with the management of the organisation.

A specialist consultant, however, is offering not only a capability but a facility to advise an organisation in a particular way, which may include aspects from development of a strategy in a given field through to ultimate implementation of the agreed recommendations. The main difference, we suggest, is that the organisation in this instance is a *client* of the consultant, whereas the organisation is more the *employer* of the contractor, buying hours rather than specialist knowledge or advice. There is, of course, a grey area in between, and some of our former management consulting colleagues carrying out routine tasks for certain organisations would be horrified if we were to classify them as self-employed contractors rather than management consultants. It is important, though, for you to decide which of these two ways of working you wish to adopt, because it will determine your whole approach to setting yourself up in a new framework and positioning yourself to make a success of it.

We have described above the main steps necessary to establish a home office and to operate as a self-employed contractor; becoming a specialist consultant is, however, a much more complex matter. We suggest that the following steps should be considered if that is the path to be taken:

- **Think carefully about your capability**, since you will need to be focused in your approach, both in terms of promoting yourself and selecting a given market sector in which to operate initially. More importantly, as emphasised elsewhere, you should spend time considering *what you really want to do* rather than attempting to continue much of what you have been doing already. For example, both the authors forsook the general consulting roles held previously to specialise in areas which were significantly different, but made use of the skills and experience built up over many years as professional management consultants. It is therefore vital that you should get under your skin and discover the underlying motivations that you can draw upon to make a new venture a success. In examining your own capability, therefore, you will need to consider, for example, whether it is your *training capability* that is most relevant, or your *technical knowledge*, or your *analytical* or *interpersonal skills*, or your *marketing familiarity* with a given sector. There are many dimensions to your capability, and the outputs from time spent considering the various possibilities and preferences should prove well worthwhile.

- **Determine your chosen market**, related to the outcome of your thinking about the aspects of your capability which you believe to be both desirable and marketable. It will naturally be easiest if you are able to choose an industry sector, or small group of sectors, for marketing a narrow specialist activity. On the other hand, many specialisms apply across a range of sectors – for example, *energy management*. This could be termed a narrow specialism (you wouldn't attempt it, we suggest, unless you had been much involved before!) but it is applicable to any firm that spends above a certain sum on energy costs across all sectors, including the public sector. Also *project management* and various *human resources* requirements apply to all sectors, so you have to be selective in the potential client population you choose.

You may decide that it is only large corporations and multinationals that you will tackle initially, but don't forget that nearly every other business attempts this route and you would be competing with the best in the land! You therefore have to have a strong justification to merit your choice of initial target population.

A prominent feature in any buying situation (and we speak from experience as purchasers of consultancy projects) is the response to the question *'Where have you done this before?'*. If the answer is 'Well, I haven't actually done this before, but I'm sure I could cope' you are on to a loser, but if you can point to specific experience that is directly applicable you will stand a good chance of getting the job.

Most consultancy projects these days are bought on a competitive basis, and the two single attributes that normally determine the outcome are the *knowledge and integrity* of the consultant(s) concerned and their *past experience* in the fields to be covered. This aspect presents a new consultant with a difficult task, since no one wants to be restricted in this way by previous experience – it is for this reason that we suggest you may wish to consider linking up with others who possess complementary skills and experience. It is possible to join up with a variety of networks, from just linking up on an informal basis with a couple of friends to becoming part of a larger, established network or an associate of a major consulting firm. This is why it is so important for you to be clear about what you actually have to offer, and who might therefore be sufficiently interested in your skills and experience to pay for your services – very basic thoughts, but a realistic assessment at the start can save a great deal of heartache in the future!

- **Draw up a marketing plan** based on the above considerations. This should, in our view, be worked out in much detail and should itemise the prospects (the people in the given target firms) that you are intending to tackle during the first year, with targets set for the consultancy projects that you hope to sell and operate during that period.

  An essential feature in this planning process, we believe, is the development of a simple brochure which will outline your offerings and capability to a prospective client. This activity will highlight, if it hasn't been evident before, the need for you to define your *consultancy products*. Marketing only a capability is insufficient, we believe, to satisfy potential buyers, because they need help to understand quickly what you are about. You have to think of this aspect in their terms, too, or they will tend to brush you aside. Our advice, therefore, is to describe your offerings as straightforwardly as possible, using words that are readily understood by the market sector you are addressing. There is no substitute for testing this out with one or two friendly executives before you go too far – people are usually only too willing to help if you ask in the right way. The simple device of forcing yourself to set out your wares in a brochure – which needn't be glossy or expensive – we regard as one of the single most important steps in the successful launch of a new consulting business, since it is your face to the world.

- **Develop an appropriate business plan** as an extension of the marketing plan. We have suggested focusing on marketing first, because we believe that consideration of products and markets should be the bedrock of the new venture and that, having convinced yourself about what is feasible, you should now explore in some depth the financial implications of operating as a specialist consultant.

  One of the main tasks will be to determine what your pricing policy should be. A simple rule of thumb in a professional firm is that your personal fee rate should be three times what you earn as a salary; as a sole practitioner, with low overheads but quite a bit of non-fee-earning involved, it is not unreasonable to set a fee rate at twice what you would expect to earn in your plan. You should also ask around to find out what individual consultants are charging in practice, so that you can determine a minimum fee rate for your initial phase, when you might well be prepared to operate at a discounted rate in return for obtaining those first few projects which are so vital for success. Consultancy is not generally bought mainly on price, however, and you should not expect a high level of take-up if you drop the price to a very low degree – it just doesn't work like that.

Perhaps a few figures would help to clarify things a little. Say that you hoped to earn £50,000 as a salary in a year, or in 220 potentially active days excluding holidays, etc. If you were to consider overheads of, say, £30,000, and a utilisation of only 50 per cent (allowing considerable time for selling and administration), you would need to cover £80,000 costs in 110 days, which is equivalent to a fee rate of £727 per day. From consideration of these basic assumptions you can vary the amounts to arrive at a fee rate that you will feel comfortable with. Some people would be content with operating at a fee rate of £250 per day, particularly if they are working for an associate firm that has sold the work, while others would never take on anything at less than £1,000 per day.

So there is a range of potential fee rates that could be a viable proposition – you will have to decide what is most appropriate for you in your specific situation.

Once the fee and overhead amounts have been determined, therefore, it should be possible to set out the cash flow implications and make an assessment of the funding implications. The best situation to be in, of course, is one in which a partial or early pension covers the basic living costs so that the additional funding requirements are minimal. If this is not the case it will be necessary to explore the potential contributions that could be made by a bank, family or friend – the really essential feature is to work out the likely cash flow projections under various circumstances.

We strongly recommend three sets of calculations based on the best, worst and average forecasts – and then assess your funding requirements on the worst situation. If you go through these steps then you are unlikely to stray too far from the straight and narrow, but do please talk through your business plan with a knowledgeable friend or adviser before you finalise things. We recommend that you write up your business plan formally even if you don't require external finance – it should help you to convince yourself that it represents a sound proposition which will merit your undivided attention in the coming months, and is something against which you will be able to monitor future performance.

- **Start up your venture**, which you can either do quietly or with a bang! A launch is a potentially valuable opportunity to let prospective clients and friends know that you are now operational and are offering specific consultancy services in the market place. So you could, if you considered it to be worthwhile, hold a launch event in the form of a reception in a presentable venue, and invite a guest of honour to say a few words. Such an event provides a focus to your initial activities through, for example, preparation of an invitation list of prospects – your initial database – and a target date for your publicity material. However, you may already have clients that have signed up with you before you left your main job, and, as a launch event costs money, you may decide to leave things a while and celebrate on your first anniversary when more funds are available!

The authors both speak passionately about one particular aspect that has to be sorted out if you are to be successful, and that is the thorny subject of finance and administration. You may choose to carry out the work involved entirely by yourself, and if you really are proficient in these areas (and don't mind spending the time on it) then that's fine. But most of us find such tasks irksome, even if we claim to be competent and can discipline ourselves to carry them out, and the norm in this situation is that everything eventually gets behind and no one knows quite what is happening, let alone what is the exact financial situation at any one time. So our advice is to use the assistance of someone who can administer your business and keep the books; a mature person living locally and working part-time would be the ideal solution. The real difficulty is that working for clients should be the priority, and if you are successful you will neither have the time nor the interest for the somewhat tedious, though essential, routine tasks. If you get it wrong you will be in danger of losing good clients and prevented from taking on new ones – people are not prepared to tolerate rampant inefficiency for long. So do please be realistic and decide to delegate finance and administrative tasks if at all possible – we have found in our Third Age careers that a smooth office machine is disproportionately important, and our research findings reinforce our comments on the difficulty, surprisingly, of getting it right.

Operating as a consultant rather than as an employee may be difficult at first for some, but it should be remembered that working within an organisation is very often in practice like working for different sets of internal clients. It may therefore be less strange than anticipated, but the priority will be to ensure that the consultant-client relationship is sound, based on a clear professional understanding. Without going into this aspect in any depth, we suggest that the following topics should be considered in some detail by the consultant if the business is to be viable:

- **The prospecting and selling process**, making the best use of time and reaching the heart of the matter as swiftly and effectively as possible.

- **The formal proposal**, which should be a document that clearly outlines the terms of reference for a given project or assignment, the work to be carried out, the programme and projected timescale, the fee cost involved and the stated terms of business. All these aspects are essential since it is in essence a contract that you are drawing up, even if only in the form of a letter for a limited engagement.

- **Clarifying the relationship** once the project has been started up. It is important to identify exactly who is the client – it should be a person rather than a Board or Working Party – and to agree regular meetings to review progress. In many situations it is helpful to nominate someone in the client organisation who would be the link person to make the necessary arrangements and to facilitate all appropriate relationships.

- **Develop a continuing relationship with the client**, in an appropriate way, through and beyond the particular project you are undertaking. Organisations tend to welcome a relationship with a consultant that is marked by mutual trust and can be switched on and off as required, but they abhor a pushy consultant who hangs on and is insensitive to the organisation's situation. We have known situations in which an organisation has resolved never to use a specific consultant again because of unwarranted sales pressure at the end of a given assignment.

- **Engage in some form of continuing professional development** to ensure that you keep up to date and learn about advanced technological or business management practices. This may be achieved, for example, through membership of the Institute of Management Consultants, or through attending appropriate courses at a university or business school, or participating in some of the many conferences that are widely advertised in consultancy journals. If you are working in association with a group of other consultants, regular away days can be a valuable form of continuing professional development, through sharing assignment experiences and developing joint solutions to specific issues raised. You may also wish to participate in the regular Consulting Skills seminars organised by Maresfield Curnow (0171 435 0592)

3. Fulfilling the Role of Non-Executive Director

In our experience there is a considerable degree of mythology about (a) the desirability and (b) the practicality of becoming a non-executive director. We have received countless requests in Future Perfect for introductions that are perceived should result in immediate directorial appointments, and some executives glibly talk about 'getting a string of NEDs' as the heart of their preferred Third Age plan. For anyone who is thinking in this way we would like to remove these illusions by stating a few hard facts:

- **Reputable companies would not even consider you unless you had had significant Board experience already.**

- **There is an oversupply of potential candidates for any NED appointment.**

- **The legal requirements for a NED are exactly the same as for an executive director and thus a NED carries significant responsibilities.**

- **It is therefore no sinecure, and selection as a NED of a reputable company is by no means easy to achieve.**

There has been a considerable amount of change in the corporate governance field in recent years, notably through the Cadbury Report but also in terms of Boards realising that they have to specify the sort of person they need and defining particular roles for them. It involves very much more than attending regular Board meetings, since an understanding of such aspects as relevant business activities and employee attitudes is clearly beneficial to effective stewardship in the NED role.

Having said that, and you are not put off, becoming a NED can be a very satisfying activity, to which many Third Agers will testify. If you have the necessary Board experience to qualify – and we regard knowledge of Board/Company procedures to be important in this context – you will need to consider how best to achieve a satisfactory appointment. There are a number of avenues which we believe that you should explore:

- **Your personal network**, through which you should obviously let it be known that you would be available for NED appointments, specifying your particular strengths and aspirations. Personal influence is still, we suggest, an important factor in the recruitment of NEDs in British companies.

- **Recruitment agencies**, concentrating on headhunting firms with whom you may have a relationship or applying to specialist agencies such as Hanson Green (0171 493 0837) or PRO NED (0171 240 8305). A well-presented personal profile and clear statement of what you are after would naturally be helpful in these circumstances. They will obviously follow up your enquiry with a much more detailed questionnaire if they consider that you would be suitable, but it is wise to remember that you will need to 'sell yourself' throughout this process.

- **Carry out relevant research**, which is what we advise most people to do if they wish to pursue this route. The greatest need for effective NEDs lies with small to medium-sized companies, and we suggest that you should research the companies that (a) are local to you and (b) are in the industry sectors that relate to your capability. If you then draw up a short list and obtain appropriate company details you can approach those that look promising, preferably using an introductory link of some kind based on personal knowledge.

- **Approach the Cabinet Office in Whitehall** directly if your interests lie in the public sector. In the Public Appointments Unit there is a candidate register from which are drawn names of those who wish to become Health Authority Board members, Quango directors or any other public appointment. Anyone can apply to be included in this register, and you should write for a nomination form to: The Director, Public Appointments Unit, Cabinet Office, Horse Guards Road, London SW1P 3AL. Before taking this step, however, it would be advisable for you to assess whether or not your qualifications and other personal qualities would fit you for such roles.

In conclusion, therefore, we would just say that a NED appointment can be a highly satisfying role for the right people, and they are normally, in our experience, people who are extremely hard-working and are almost fanatical in their enthusiasm about business. Many are well into their Third Age and find it gives them a continuing stimulus which they believe they would be unable to obtain in any other way. It is our perception that the role of NED is far more demanding than most people imagine, and actually needs the breed of workaholics who can make such a valuable contribution by using their skills and experience in this way.

4. Starting Up a New Manufacturing or Service Business With Others

It is not sufficiently appreciated, we believe, that you can minimise the potential threat of redundancy or 'ageism' by setting up your own business, and then running it for as long as you like – until you are 60,

70 or even 80! There are quite a number of people working for medium or large companies who would much prefer to 'run their own show', and for such people there is a significant opportunity to grasp the nettle and turn a pipe dream into a reality at an appropriate juncture, probably when they are in their 40s. One of the authors (as a director of a company called Science Cities) has been heavily involved in this field for many years, assisting with the development of small businesses in technoparks and with the creation of new businesses in sponsored regional business venture programmes. Based on this experience, therefore, we would at the outset advise that a cautious approach be taken to starting on this path; it is likely to require a much higher level of commitment than many of the other options, but can be much more rewarding in both financial and self-fulfilment terms. It all goes back to what you really want out of life, and we suggest that the successful business professionals who will make a good fist of it are likely to have the following particular qualities:

- **They want to be rich**; they want to be visibly successful and to be able to buy the things that go with a materially successful lifestyle.

- **They really enjoy business life**; they tend to 'live to work rather than work to live' and get a real kick out of being involved in a business and achieving sound business results, particularly through new initiatives that they have personally masterminded.

- **They are decisive**; they are prepared to take the necessary decisions to achieve the best possible outcome, even if they are unpopular.

- **They are energetic**; they have the sort of energy, commitment and leadership qualities that will carry them through difficult times, which will inevitably occur.

In other words, we are saying that you shouldn't even attempt to go along this route if you cannot identify with the above characteristics.

Perhaps we can illustrate this aspect by describing our experience with a specific programme, the Business Venture Programme sponsored by the Glasgow Development Agency and Scottish Enterprise and launched in 1993. Managers who wished to start up a new business were recruited in batches of 25, were trained in small business management through a 10-week programme, and were offered the opportunity of linking up with successful businesses in North America (who wished to enter Europe) to form a new joint enterprise. This has been a highly effective, though relatively expensive, programme and has created new businesses at the rate of one a month. One feature, however, that emerged from this experience was that only 50 per cent of the venturers ever got as far as putting their money on the table and actually taking the risk of committing themselves to a new venture. How much better it would have been if those who were ultimately never going to take those steps had not started off in the first place!

Despite careful screening it was not possible to make an objective external assessment that was at all accurate (to our surprise), which is why we strongly advise you to look at yourself again and make your own, balanced judgement about the characteristics we have highlighted. We found that a frequent stumbling block arose when the person concerned finally explained to their partner that it would be necessary to put all their assets into the business to get it off the ground initially – one person actually pulled out of an agreed business partnership just days before the projected launch. So it really is worthwhile to check out aspects such as these early on; a business of your own, normally as part of a team, will affect those around you to a considerable degree, and the backing of a supportive family is highly desirable!

Given those personal attributes, the next most important factor is having a realistic business proposition to pursue – and many already have this up their sleeve when they approach this consideration. There are, however, an increasing number of programmes similar to the Business Venture Programme in Glasgow that are providing participants with relevant business ideas and opportunities – so if the desire is there it should still be possible to join up with others to launch a soundly-based new business.

We therefore list below the various aspects that will need to be considered, and advice taken on if necessary, before a new venture can become a reality – it will normally take between six months and a year, depending on the nature of the venture.

Working as a team

This is one of the most important ingredients for a successful outcome. We very much recommend a team approach if the business is to rise above the results achieved by a limited one-person entrepreneurial arrangement. It therefore follows that members of the team should get along well with each other and should be mutually supportive. They should also possess complementary skills and experience wherever possible – a trio of a marketing, a finance and an operations person is normally a viable combination. You can, however, buy in specific skills, and we believe that acceptable personal qualities and a feeling of mutual trust are more important than specific technical skills.

How do you find suitable partners, then? You may be fortunate enough to be part of a cohesive breakaway unit from a larger firm, but that seems to be the exception rather than the rule. You may also search your personal network of business contacts, and then approach those you trust and would be prepared to work closely with. Beyond that we suggest that you look around for appropriate programmes (like the one in Glasgow we referred to earlier) to provide a suitable forum for meeting and assessing people in the new business context; the DTI's Business Links initiative may be able to help you find the right vehicle.

When it comes down to it, though, you have to take the initiative and make your own choice of programme and then people – no one is going to do it for you. On the Glasgow programme we spent many hours nurturing potential relationships to assist with this process so that the individuals involved would be able to make their own judgements based on seeing people in a variety of situations – being part of a project team, participating in the workshop forum, attending a formal dinner with speaker, socialising until the early hours over several drinks or meeting privately away from the group. It is not dissimilar to courting, since the resulting partnership is likely to be of life-enhancing (or threatening) significance over many years and therefore merits priority attention. We would say that the make-up of a team is vastly more important than the nature of the business proposition. Given that the plan successfully undergoes the usual rigorous business analysis and funding processes, it is the team that will make it succeed; a good team will normally make a success of whatever it decides to tackle.

Marketing

This is the next most important feature of the business proposition. In the initial stages the product or service profiles will not normally be fully developed, though products from other countries may be close to a final version. The critical factor is to gain a realistic market assessment of whatever is proposed without indulging in a full-blown market research project, which would be both time-consuming and expensive.

Competent desk research is absolutely essential, and there is no better way than testing out such a proposition than by doing it yourself – but you may be fortunate enough to have access to appropriate professional assistance. In addition, we strongly recommend that you should, wherever possible, test out the product or service concept directly with potential customers on a pilot basis, and be prepared to listen to what they are telling you. It is all too easy to be swept off your feet with what you have to offer and discard the reservations that are expressed, and a languishing business is the result. We would almost go further and suggest that this process (which should ideally progress beyond a pilot stage) should lead to a number of provisional orders after the potential customer has declared 'If you actually do that I will be prepared to take up your first offerings when you start the new business'.

You should never make assumptions based solely on your own opinions; we have known too many situations in which businesses have failed through lack of a market 'want' despite imaginative concepts and worthwhile products. The potential viability has to come from an objective assessment of the likely penetration of the target markets identified and the volume of business which is realistically likely to emerge from them. Success in another country, or imitation of a successful model in your own country, is no indication that your products or services will receive similar acclamation – it needs testing out.

Business planning and funding

Once the team is satisfied that their business proposition is basically sound, business planning and funding are the next essential steps, which we have combined because they go hand in hand with each other. Funding institutions demand that a carefully constructed business plan be prepared if they are to consider an application seriously, and it is therefore necessary to be aware of their requirements right from the start. It is also advisable to determine at an early stage which sources of finance, and the amounts involved, are likely to be a realistic possibility. As most people will be aware, the finance may arise from two or more of the following sources:

- The business team – each member should contribute significantly, we suggest
- Development Agency, involving grants or loans supported by European or local government funding
- Commercial bank, normally in the form of a loan
- Venture capital company, normally in terms of equity participation
- Venture capitalists, of which there are many looking for a sound investment
- Business contacts who would be prepared to support the team and may take on a non-executive role to assist in achieving a good return on their investment.

Each of these sources, and the proportions of funding allocated, should be considered very carefully because the resulting interest payments might, for example, jeopardise the cash flow implications in the early stages to an alarming degree if the projected results take longer to materialise than forecast. It goes without saying that the cash flow projections, and subsequent monitoring of the outcome, are the most critical feature in managing a small new business. It is therefore advisable to minimise any funding that has burdensome short-term commitments; it is the long-term growth of the business that should appeal to investors and it is our belief that there are more individuals prepared to back such new ventures than is generally realised. Formal networks exist in different parts of the country, in addition to personal acquaintances, and this source can be very attractive in comparison with commercial banks, which are naturally looking for an ongoing, short-term return.

All the above features, and much more, need to be incorporated in a formal business planning document. Though its formulation (and repeated amendments) can be somewhat demanding, the process is actually very beneficial in that it provides a focus for any discussion on the potential future of the business. It is not just a plan, it represents the conclusions reached by the business partners after much research and deliberation and it is the prospectus for potential investors or lenders – it may be the only visible part of the new venture in the early stages before a funding package has been put together and final approval given.

It would be inappropriate for us to elaborate at length on the business planning process in this book, but we thought that it might be helpful, as an outline guide, to list the typical contents of a business plan:

1. **Introduction**, setting out the history and basis for the new business venture.

2. **The issues and the market opportunity**, going into further detail about the products or services to be offered to meet a perceived market need.

3. **The business strategy**, explaining clearly the logic of entering into the chosen market with the products and services described, outlining the methods to be used in production, sales and distribution, and setting out the financial implications behind the proposal.

4. **Market obstacles and competition**, demonstrating a sharp understanding, based on research, of the current market situation and how the new venture will be able to take advantage of a particular market niche, in quantified terms.

5. **Organisation and management**, describing how the new business will be organised, the roles of the partners and of the people they intend to employ as the business grows on the basis of the plan.

6. **Financial implications**, setting out in considerable detail the financial projections for the business for the next three years, with cash flow projections being a key element of this information.

7. **The proposal**, in summary form, for potential investors or funders, demonstrating a satisfactory return, even under a pessimistic scenario (we normally favour the inclusion of a best, worst and reasonable case somewhere in the document).

The legal status and equity participation details would naturally also be included. Detailed calculations, etc., should form suitable Appendices to the document.

Model business plans exist, and they can normally be obtained from business development agencies or relevant financial institutions. It is not necessary to follow a rigid format, however, since the main external purpose is to tell a credible story which will support in factual terms the verbal proposition put forward by the venturer partners. It should therefore be easily readable, and should be such as to persuade any reader to invest their own money in the venture – which is always the ultimate test for any business proposition.

Launching and running the business

Following acceptance of the business plan by all the parties concerned, the next stage is put the plan into effect and launch the business. It is perhaps not generally appreciated that the launch of a new business provides unique potential for PR visibility – it is an opportunity that won't occur again! Full advantage should therefore be taken to optimise this opportunity by mounting an event – which needn't be elaborate or expensive – for business associates and potential customers, and using that occasion as a focus for appropriate media publicity. Such an event forces the main participants to sharpen up their message and to construct an initial database that will form the basis for an ongoing marketing programme. Beyond that, in running the business day-to-day, there is no substitute for energetic and dedicated application of all the skills and experience that has led the participants to this juncture!

5. Working For the Community or For a Charity

Many participants in Future Perfect workshops have said that they feel they would now 'like to give something back' after a life and career that has treated them relatively kindly. Others have said that they 'would like to leave a legacy' – presumably something for which they would be remembered favourably. Though these may be very vague aspirations at that stage they do, we believe, form the powerful germ of a latent intention which could lead to imaginative and fulfilling activities for those courageous enough to pursue that vague aspiration further.

Perhaps we could first explore the benefits of taking the 'charitable' route before considering exactly how this type of opportunity can be researched and acted upon. Speaking from personal experience, one of the authors has become heavily involved with a charity as part of his 'portfolio' in recent years, and has been surprised by the rewarding nature of the work. It might therefore be helpful to illustrate the pros and cons of the charitable opportunity by examining this personal experience in some depth. It is, however, difficult to put into words, but the sequence of events and activities involved were as follows:

At the back of my mind I had a feeling that I wanted to expand or diversify my 'portfolio' to include something completely different, something far away from my experiences to date. I also felt that I wanted it to be 'people' oriented.

One day I was browsing in a bookshop in Covent Garden and noticed a book by someone called David Rees. I used to know a David Rees at Cambridge who had read English, and to my astonishment I discovered that the book in question was the same David Rees's autobiography! What is more, when I read the book I found a reference to myself when he wrote about life in college. Having neither seen nor heard of him since those days I wrote to him via the publisher to see whether we might be able to meet up again. Sadly I received a brief note from a friend of his some while later saying that David was, in fact, dying of AIDS in a London Hospice. I went to see him, and it had a profound effect on me.

After mulling things over for a while I thought that the HIV/AIDS field might be one through which I could fulfil my vague charitable aspirations and do something completely different. I must confess that I was very apprehensive, though, when I started out on this path and visited my first AIDS agency to explore the possibilities. It was certainly very different from the business scenarios I was used to!

Eventually I was introduced to the Globe Centre in East London, was vetted and started training as a volunteer in early 1994. The training programme was a remarkable experience, a real eye-opener. I was very impressed with the training itself and with the experience of sharing so much with people from a variety of walks of life – all much younger than me!

I became a volunteer in 'Day Care' for one day a week (when I could), helping to look after service users at the Centre. Unfortunately it became known in due course that I was a management consultant by profession, and I somewhat reluctantly became Chair of the Board of Trustees in late 1995.

The above comments summarise a process that took some two to three years to gel, but it was interesting for the author (and hopefully the reader) to appreciate how the pattern emerged and how this 'career opportunity' has been connected to personal life events. It would be easy to say 'that's not my scene' in almost any instance, yet it is our belief that, if the deeper motivation is there, it is possible to flourish in the most unexpected situations.

So what are the pros and cons of working for a charity, based on this experience? The following would seem to be relevant:

Cons
- Earning no money; even if direct expenses are recovered, it can still be a costly activity.

- A frustration that things aren't run as efficiently run as you would like and are accustomed to.

- The priority need to raise money for the charity in an increasingly competitive climate; it is an unwelcome, but essential, function.

Pros

- A sense of belonging to a group of friendly people who are doing something worthwhile.

- Meeting new people from all walks of life.

- A feeling that you are valued and that your skills and experience are being put to good use.

- The rewarding experience of direct personal contact with those for whom the charity exists.

These are fairly general points which could apply, we suggest, in almost any charity situation. The surprising outcome to the author was the degree to which it became a two-way benefit – it is not really about 'giving something back', it is about 'getting something new' and fulfilling a part of your life that you probably didn't realise existed until you started out on that path. It is important, therefore, that you should address the charity potential in an imaginative way if you want to end up in the right place. The following steps are suggested:

- From your self-knowledge exploration try to determine what are your deeper motivations that might be put to charitable effect, e.g. if you are a compassionate person a caring agency would be appropriate or, if you feel strongly about the environment, an organisation focused on a particular feature might be suitable. You do, however, need to feel fairly passionately about the topic. If you consider that you don't really feel passionate about anything, then perhaps you haven't quite looked at yourself long or deeply enough! Most people feel strongly about children (if you are stuck) and there are many charities connected with the welfare of young people, covering homelessness, child abuse, illness, family life, etc., both nationally and locally.

- Having started to define the areas in which you might like to operate, you will need to undertake a considerable amount of research. It is best to go to a local library to investigate every possible source of relevant information, because it is both local and national organisations that you will need to consider – and there are thousands of them (about 170,000 registered charities in the UK)! The *Charities Digest* is published annually by the Family Welfare Association. This is a useful volume but cannot, of course, cover all the possibilities. Reviewing the opportunities, though, in whatever form the information may be obtainable, should enable you to firm up some ideas about the sort of charity you might like to work for and what sort of activity you might be prepared to carry out (which we believe to be a secondary consideration, because there is usually a great deal of flexibility about the roles one can perform).

- Alternatively, you could adopt an entirely different approach and decide to offer your services through an agency, such as REACH (Retired Executives Action Clearing House), Bear Wharf, 27 Bankside, London SE1 9ET (0171 928 0452) and see what comes up. We believe that it is preferable, however, to have a relatively clear idea of your priorities before approaching them – but it is an excellent channel through which to explore genuine opportunities, because each job opportunity on REACH's books represents a real, and probably urgent, need.

  Two other agencies which should also be considered, particularly if overseas activities are of appeal, are VSO and BESO. VSO (Voluntary Service Overseas) enables men and women to work alongside poorer people in poorer countries in order to share skills, build capabilities and promote international understanding and action in the pursuit of a more equitable world. Volunteers are normally committed to a project for at least two years, and mainstream examples include Education, Health, Natural Resources, Business, and Social Development. If you are interested you should write to: VSO Enquiries Unit, 317 Putney Bridge Road, London SW15 2PN (0181 780 1331).

  BESO (British Executives Service Overseas) helps meet the needs of deserving enterprises and organisations in the developing world by providing worthwhile and sustainable assistance from volunteers who undertake short-term advisory, consultancy and training assignments. Assignments can last from two weeks to six months, and all travel and living expenses are covered for the adviser and spouse, plus a small allowance on top. These are ideal opportunities for offering your skills and experience in another country, assuming that you are able to travel and be away from home for the period of time indicated. If interested, you should write to: The Director, BESO, 164 Vauxhall Bridge Road, London SW1V 2RB (0171 630 0644).

• Taking the output from the charity research indicated, it is appropriate to write to one of the agencies referred to or to the Chair of the Trustees or the Director of a given short list of charities expressing an interest in their activities. You should ask for a meeting to explore the potential opportunity for assistance – and you will find that you will normally be greeted with open arms.

• An introductory visit should then occur and it will be important for you to assess your reactions during and after the occasion. You will probably be surprised by the somewhat primitive working conditions, but, having overcome any reservations on that score, you should examine your feelings about the charity itself, about its Director and staff, the overall level of commitment observed, and the financial and organisational situation. If doubts emerge then you should be extremely cautious.

• Assuming that you are able to find a charity and an accompanying role which suits you, you should ensure that you undergo an appropriate induction process. A number of charities have relevant volunteer training programmes, and participation in one of these can be an invaluable experience. From then on it is up to you to make what you can of the opportunity – it will not be like working for a conventional business organisation, and in our experience a successful outcome will depend significantly on personal initiative and flexibility in responding to given situations. You will probably need to get rid of your previous paradigms to make a go of it!

In summary, there is a wide range of interesting opportunities for potential Third Agers in working for a local or national charity which is barely recognised by the majority of business and professional people. Once the person concerned is linked up with a charity they wonder why they had not done this before and why many of their friends and associates have similarly missed out on such opportunities. Possibly the traditional theme of either earning money (working like stink) or being retired (not working, and enjoying relaxation) has become too deeply embedded for this mid-course activity to become a reality. We encourage you to try the approach out for yourself – you won't be disappointed.

In addition to working for specific charities, the opportunities for becoming a Justice of the Peace (via the Lord Chancellor's Department), a school governor, a local authority councillor, or a community worker of some kind fall into this category. They are perhaps the more obvious outlets for a community spirit, and it is likely that those who actually pursue that route will already have forged appropriate links during the course of their main career, which can then be developed to fruition at this subsequent stage.

One particular opportunity for Third Agers that is relatively new is presented by the practice of **family mediation**, which is being increasingly used to support the legal processes involved in cases of separation and divorce. There has been quite a bit of publicity about family mediation in connection with the Family Bill, but few appear to appreciate the nature of the function and the capability that is required. For this reason we are repeating the following from the leaflet of the National Family Mediation Association entitled 'What does Family Mediation mean?', which helps to give an appropriate insight.

'Family mediation is a process in which an impartial third person, the mediator, assists those involved in family breakdown to make arrangements following separation or divorce, to communicate better and to reach their own agreed joint decisions. The issues to be decided may concern the divorce, the separation, the children, finance and property. The mediator has no stake in the dispute, is not identified with any of the competing interests and has no power to impose a settlement on the participants, who retain authority to make their own decisions.

The principle that decision-making authority rests with the participants is fundamental to mediation. Mediators respect the participants' authority to make decisions even in circumstances of stress and upheaval. Consequently their perceptions and values are taken into full consideration. It is this principle that distinguishes mediation from other dispute resolution processes such as lawyer negotiation, litigation and adjudication. Additional essential principles of mediation are voluntariness of participation, confidentiality of exchanges and the impartiality of the mediator. Furthermore the principle of "procedural flexibility" available to the mediator provides the opportunity for the expression by the participants of the unique historical, emotional, ethical and other aspects of their situation.

These principles of mediation are designed to protect the fairness and integrity of the process as well as the interests of the participants – their dignity, needs, privacy, exchanges and self-determination and the best interests of all family members, especially the children.'

If you are interested in training as a mediator you should contact the Association at 9 Tavistock Place, London WC1H 9SN (0171 383 5993). Training is provided nationally over a period of six months, which will include two residential training weekends and four regional training days. This really is an excellent opportunity for a professional person who would like to branch out and do something different.

6. Learning New Skills or Enhancing Knowledge in a Chosen Field

The Third Age represents a once-in-a-lifetime chance of catching up on learning aspirations that have been around for a very long while. Many people have had their earlier, academic years interrupted or diverted by having to earn money relatively quickly, or to marry and bring up children. The hunger for learning has generally remained with them, though lying under the surface, and there are others who have only recognised their desire to acquire new knowledge later on in life.

A remarkable feature, however, is the extent to which this thirst for education has materialised in practice; mature students in academic institutions are now a significant part of the student population. We have been astonished at the dedication and commitment of some mature people who have pursued demanding courses over several years, particularly with bodies such as the Open University. The level of personal fulfilment from achieving a new qualification, or an ordinary or second degree, is undoubtedly exceptional if we are to believe the enthusiastic comments of those involved. Many appear to find a great deal of satisfaction from the learning process itself, rather than the ultimate achievement resulting from participation in the programme. Women in particular seem to value the experience of doing something purely for themselves (rather than their family) and enjoy to the full the camaraderie involved in being a student again.

How does one recognise this longing in oneself, though? We suggest that it might emerge from a desire to do something different, but not being quite sure what that might be. Entering a training programme of some kind, whether academic or of a more practical nature, is an excellent step towards giving life a new perspective. Many then find that it leads them to take fresh initiatives which they otherwise would not have considered. You should not discount the benefit of the personal interaction with others on the course, and the feeling of belonging to an intimate group (as part of the larger unit, the college) which is highly prized. So, when this is being considered as one of your options, please don't neglect the surrounding advantages of academic life – the qualification you are aiming for may be much less significant than you at first thought!

The learning opportunities throughout the UK are almost limitless. Again, thorough research into the possibilities in your area is an essential task, and a local library should provide relevant information on university, college and other programmes covering everything from short courses lasting only weeks to degree courses taking several years to complete. Asking colleagues or friends can also reveal personal recommendations which could make a difference – paper information alone can be somewhat unsatisfactory. Having chosen a subject, though, it becomes easier to draw up a short list of possibilities, which will then require following up through visits and interviews.

It is difficult to offer advice on the actual focus for learning since everyone will have different interests and aspirations. Possibly it might be helpful to list the topics which have generally been chosen by Third Agers since they tend to fall into one of the following categories:

Artistic academic

Art history of some kind is quite a favourite subject, since it frequently represents a furtherance of personal interest for which time has now become available – it is a natural progression for those belonging to cultural groups such as NADFAS (which candidates might also wish to join if they are not yet members). This can be combined with travel to museums and art galleries across the world.

Pure academic

There are a number of people who had always wanted to study history, English literature or similar and now realise that a golden opportunity to do this has actually materialised.

Languages

We know many people who have taken the opportunity to learn or brush up a foreign language, not just to give them a competitive edge on holiday but to enjoy an increased level of understanding of the country concerned.

Career academic

This is particularly relevant to technological areas such as IT, electronics and engineering, where individuals are looking to upgrade their knowledge in their chosen or related field. It could also apply to business school programmes; we know of one instance in which the mature student eventually ended up as a tutor on the programme! This category includes other areas, such as counselling and psychotherapy, which offers the opportunity for people to change direction.

Career practical

We are thinking here of programmes which provide tuition in necessary skills such as word processing and use of up-to-date computer and telecommunications equipment, from a basic through to an advanced stage.

Artistic practical

Many Third Agers wish to recapture the pleasure which they gained from hobbies relinquished quite a few years ago, and there are some very stimulating courses for teaching craft subjects in a very satisfying way, some being combined with a holiday in an attractive part of the world. But it could also include advanced craft programmes – in ceramics, metal or wood – for enhancing a given career or changing direction.

7. Becoming a Teacher, Counsellor, Adviser or Mentor

It is inadequately acknowledged, in most fields, that the Third Ager has a wealth of wisdom and experience that can be beneficial to others, generally those younger than themselves who are grappling with day-to-day issues under very great pressure. This wisdom, based on considerable experience of personal, family and career difficulties, and past hurdles overcome, can be harnessed in a variety of ways. We believe, however, that potential candidates for such a role have to become proactive in qualifying themselves and searching out relevant opportunities. It is unrealistic to expect that people will beat a path to your door, having become mysteriously aware that you available for consultation.

Both the authors are advisers/mentors in different areas, and it might perhaps be helpful to outline our experience in a very specific field to illustrate the sort of approach to engagement which we see to be relevant for this activity. In a particular situation, one of the authors wanted to fulfil the role of spiritual adviser or 'soul friend' to those who might wish to avail themselves of the opportunity (traditionally termed 'spiritual direction', a complete misnomer). But how does one start this from almost a zero point, with no reputation, no qualifications and virtually nil experience? The steps taken over several years have been as follows:

- **Training** with an appropriate body was the first stage in the process, but it was anything but straightforward to find, and then be accepted by, a suitable organisation. The interview that preceded acceptance on the course was one of the most penetrating that the candidate had ever undergone, being quite different from those experienced in business life. It was somewhat startling that the basis for the interview – personal faith and life experience – ascribed values to attributes and experience that were almost directly opposed to lifestyle patterns familiar in a commercial existence. This pointed to an interesting future collaboration with others who had little regard for conventional 'success'.

- **Participation**, on a part-time basis, for over two years in a fascinating programme which combined intensive education in spiritual and psychological topics together with practical explorations of personal faith journeys, training in counselling skills, and hands-on practice in becoming a 'soul friend' and offering spiritual advice as appropriate. This was a rewarding experience.

- **Marketing oneself**, since no one would know that you were either qualified or available unless you were able to communicate the fact in an imaginative way. At first sight this appeared to be an insuperable obstacle, but business sense led to the development of a suitable network which could then provide, over time, suitable referrals. Rather surprisingly this has resulted in a consistent workload of a manageable number of candidates.

- **Practising** as a spiritual adviser has been a somewhat daunting and humbling experience – which any mentor, if they are honest with themselves, is normally prepared to acknowledge. It is very much a two-way experience, however, and you learn a great deal through the process and benefit from the considerable amount of effort expended. Despite the human frailty of the adviser, clients seem to gain a great deal by having someone independent from their employer who is rooting for them and who accepts them as they are. They feel valued and supported by the process, and we are of the opinion that many more business executives and related professionals could benefit from this imaginative approach, the emphasis being on life and career issues rather than the spiritual area in these instances, of course.

The above steps have been highlighted at some length because they apply to almost any opportunity in this general field. The majority of roles are based on training in counselling-type skills, which is a rapidly growing activity and the subject of many diploma and degree courses throughout the country. Consequently it is an ideal opportunity for people who are interested in personal interaction, and represents a career change (or start) for a wide range of people – particularly women, who appear take to the activity like ducks to water.

If you are interested in this area of development and wish to explore the various options in greater detail, we suggest the following approaches in each instance:

- **Teaching** itself represents a very diverse field since, in addition to schools, education colleges, business schools and universities, there are further education projects mounted by local authorities which could be very appropriate for someone after leaving their main career. There are also training organisations covering the management field, including the well-known management colleges such as Ashridge, Sundridge Park and Henley. The most important requirement is that you really *want* to teach and that you are good at it. You may have to study for a teaching diploma in certain instances, but there will be many business-type situations for which your professional qualifications, skills and experience will be more than adequate. So whatever level or subject you wish to concentrate on the opportunities exist and are worth pursuing.

- **Counselling** is the real growth area, since there is an increasing awareness that with the stresses and strains of modern life, problems will arise which benefit from some form of professional assistance. In addition, people are generally becoming more open about difficulties they are experiencing, particularly regarding personal relationships, and are more ready to be helped than were previous generations. Consequently a wide range of education courses have sprung up, and it is likely that there will be a suitable course at a college of some kind near you. If you would like to find out more about this you should start by approaching the British Association for Counselling, 1 Regent Place, Rugby CV21 2PJ (01788 578328) for their information pack. There is a booklet 'So you are thinking of becoming a Counsellor?' which is useful, and a *Directory of Training in Counselling and Psychotherapy* which provides all relevant information on training courses throughout the country – an essential reference book in our view if you are looking for a suitable course to take.

You might also consider writing to RELATE (formerly National Marriage Guidance Council), Herbert Gray College, Little Church Street, Rugby CV21 3AP (01788 73241), asking for an information pack and details of your local branch of RELATE. It could be that you might like to be sponsored by them for training as a counsellor, which is a paid job when qualified, or to assist by fulfilling a voluntary role as treasurer, chairman or whatever.

One advantage of training to operate as a counsellor is that much of it, after the initial training, would be in-service training, which enables you to learn by practising in real situations rather than just the classroom. Once fully qualified, it is possible to work either for a counselling organisation or to operate from appropriate counselling accommodation in your home or separate premises. This provides a level of flexibility not often available in most forms of employment. The financial reward can also be quite satisfactory; a fee rate of £25 to £30 for a one-hour session is not unreasonable. We have known countless people who have trained as counsellors in mature life and have found it to be an extremely satisfying experience; if you are genuinely interested in people it is certainly worth trying.

- **Advising** is a more general term which can apply to a wide variety of situations, including that of a 'soul friend' referred to earlier. It is principally making good use of your skills and experience in appropriate ways, frequently resulting from the network of colleagues and acquaintances gained during your main career. It could be on a one-to-one basis, or it could be as a member of committee, project team or tribunal, making full use of your special expertise. There are many occasions in organisational life when the question is asked 'Who knows about X?' and heads are scratched – if you ensure that a sufficient number of people know about your readiness to advise on a given matter, you could become quite busy. One problem, however, is that many people and organisations are looking for, and expect, free advice – if money is important then you have to be more proactive and, in effect, to set up a business, as described in Section 2 on page 131.

- **Mentoring** is a relatively new activity, which is principally seen in the context of executive development. There are firms, such as Alexander and the European Mentoring Centre, which specialise in coaching and mentoring, and client companies take on mentoring programmes to be carried out by such organisations at times of change to assist managers to become more effective and to cope with the demanding requirements of a high-powered job. Some companies operate a somewhat different form of mentoring by nominating senior executives within the company to be mentors to younger executives, seeing them from time to time and giving them the benefits of their experience. For someone leaving their main career this represents a significant opportunity (generally with your former employer but it could be a known supplier or customer) by fulfilling such a role with up and coming people in the firm. Professional people who have left their main career can be a great deal more relaxed, balanced and unbiased in their approach to life than before and can therefore be of considerable use in a mentoring role – but it requires an imaginative HR director to get such a proposition accepted. We believe that there is much scope for mentoring through networks of experienced professionals on an ongoing basis, so that the 'mentee' is able to rely on regular access to their mentor, or personal adviser, over years rather than months. The assistance given in this way could be invaluable, and in our consulting work we are promoting this theme wherever appropriate. It is closely related to counselling, since the process will deal with a range of personal issues, but it is likely to be more directional in style than pure counselling and is based more on organisational experience than qualified counselling.

8. Developing Hobbies

Initiatives for developing hobbies may be more about *rediscovering* hobbies than starting them from scratch or upgrading an ongoing activity. If you ask a busy executive what hobbies he has (apart from sport) he will usually look troubled and claim that the demands of his career never allow sufficient time for any creative activity (and how could anyone be so dim as to expect otherwise). Even reading (unconnected with a career) appears to suffer as a regular pastime, and the Third Age therefore provides the opportunity of recapturing the delights of hobbies enjoyed in the past, to whatever level of professionalism one might aspire to.

Some even develop their hobbies to the extent of turning it into a business and selling whatever they produce – we have known painters, furniture builders, computer operators, wedding cake makers, interior decorators and gardeners that have turned their capability and interest into a paid activity, yielding both a significant amount of pleasure and a financial reward.

The first step is to examine your life and, probably through closer inspection of your life map, to highlight some creative hobby that you had found satisfying early on. One of the authors realised that he used to get a great deal of pleasure from working with wood and making furniture when he was in his early teens, and that, apart from building a climbing frame for his children and constructing the odd cupboard, this hobby had been sorely neglected. This recognition was the starting point, and it eventually led to a visit to Wiston Project School in South Wales (01437 731 579) where it is possible to begin working with wood again and come away with a piece of furniture that you made yourself! This exceptionally imaginative venture is run by the Wears family, who had bought up a former village school, turned it into a woodworking facility, and used it both to restore antiques and to build new furniture. One day their solicitor asked to stay a while in the workshop because he was so fascinated by the process; he was told that he could, but that he would have to build a piece of furniture himself if he did – and so the project was born. It is difficult to describe the elegance of the furniture made by the students who come for a week or a fortnight. The pieces include, for example, a welsh dresser or settle in pine or oak, an inlaid mahogany display cabinet, a corner cupboard in American cherry or mahogany, a veneered drum table, and one of their specialities, a rocking horse. The students live in lodgings in the village while they are there, and it is quite remarkable how people with little previous experience of woodwork can produce pieces of furniture which look brilliant and become a mark of pride as they are displayed in living rooms up and down the country. The methods used are very imaginative and enable untrained workers to pick up the necessary skills within a short period of time. Advanced techniques, such as a versatile use of routers, are used to the full, which is a great advantage to have learned when working at home subsequently. One student there was so delighted with his output that he decided to make about 12 rocking horses each year and then sell them; as they retail for £1500 to £2000 this could be quite a lucrative activity! Several students have fitted out or made new workshops as a result of their visit to Wiston. So why not try out the experience yourself? – Partners are equally welcome, as they claim to be able to get a piece of furniture out of anyone!

Craft courses, therefore, are an excellent way of developing a hobby, and there are plenty of opportunities for a wide range of interests, many quite local.

You might find it worthwhile to consider accessing a suitable programme through the Open College of the Arts, which was founded in 1986 by Lord Young of Dartington and Ian Tregarthen Jenkin as a charitable trust providing home-based education in the arts; it is affiliated to the Open University. Their courses are very much hobby-oriented, and include the following subjects:

- Art and Design
- Painting
- Textiles
- Sculpture
- Drawing
- Creative Writing

- Music
- Garden Design
- Photography
- Understanding Western Art.

The College is based at Houndhill, Worsborough, Barnsley S70 6TU (01226 730495) and operates through a network of tutorial centres covering the UK; there may well be one near you. You work mainly at home, using a specially written course book, and receive regular personal support from a professional tutor, either at a local centre or by correspondence. It is a highly imaginative approach to developing hobbies – if you are interested we suggest that you ask them to send you a copy of their annual *Guide to Courses* which gives relevant details for you to explore the opportunity further.

There is another useful annual publication called *Time to Learn*, produced by the National Institute of Adult Continuing Education, 19B De Montfort Street, Leicester LE1 7GE (01533 551451). It covers not only courses at relevant centres up and down the country but also study tours in foreign parts, such as Iceland; land of ice and fire, High Pyrenees; flowers, birds and butterflies, Canada; landscape and natural history, Ireland; exploring coastal and mountain scenery.

These two publications alone should provide you with as many opportunities as you are able to cope with initially. Why not take a leap in the dark, try something new and see how you get on!

9. Sport, Travel and Leisure

Sporting activities

For the more energetic among us a firm place will undoubtedly be found for one or more sporting activities in any new 'portfolio'. Leaving a main career offers an unparalleled opportunity to engage in sport to a degree not possible since school or college days. We know of several relatively young Third Agers who play golf at least three times a week, and they look extremely well on it. It is all a question of personal choice, though, and some would actually find it tedious to spend so much time playing golf – but they might well enjoy walking, swimming, tennis, working out in the gym, fishing, riding, or sailing.

We really cannot provide any advice in this area that you are unable to develop for yourself other than to draw attention to the health benefits of physical activity, which are self-evident but frequently neglected – not least by the authors! There are some simple guidelines which you can set yourself from the health point of view, e.g. walk or cycle between events/meetings instead of driving or using public transport, go swimming at least once a week, join a local health club. If you take this suggestion seriously you will find it rewarding in the ongoing battle to lose weight and keep fit. It is better to choose something you enjoy doing rather than to be forced to use an exercise bike or to have to go to an expensive health farm every so often.

Travel

Travel is a really beneficial new opportunity if you have relinquished your main career aspirations (and your partner as well, if you have one) and are able to take a more flexible approach to life planning. Probably for the first time ever you will have the freedom to be away for more than two or three weeks and will have sufficient funds to allow for much longer journeys than you have been used to previously. Many organise round-the-world trips to visit distant relatives or to explore countries which had been only a pipedream in the past. We have been wondering how we can best inspire you to take full advantage of this opportunity, and have come up with a few unusual suggestions that you might not have heard of via the normal travel agency route:

- **Safari travel** through escorted tours in Asia and Africa by **Temple World**, 13, The Avenue, Kew, Richmond, Surrey TW9 2AL (0181 940 4114). Personally recommended, Temple World have had 25 years' experience of designing and running special interest travel, with expertise in Africa – south of the Sahara – and in Asia – Turkey, the Middle East and India. Perhaps it would be worthwhile just to list the various tours on offer to illustrate what is available:

Splendours of the Ancient Orient
– Cruising to Ephesus – the archaeology of Ionia and Caria
– The Turquoise Coast – cruising the shores of ancient Caria
– Theatres, Tombs and the Taurus – cruising through Lycia and Pamphylia
– Taking the Cross – Syria, Jordan and Lebanon
– Imperial Splendours – highlights of India and Jordan
– The Golden Triangle – Mughal India and the best of Asiatic wildlife
– Silk Road and Palaces of Rajasthan – a traveller's introduction to northern India
– The Royal Orient Express – wildlife, history and the travel of a lifetime in Gujarat

Wild Africa
– Great Elephant Safari – the Namib Desert and Etosha Pan
– Last Desert Wilderness – the Kaokoland and Himbaland of northern Namibia
– The Mighty Zambezi – Zimbabwe
– Royal Africa's Big Game – Natal and Maputaland, South Africa
– The Fairest Cape in all the World – springtime in the Cape of Good Hope
– Lost World of the Kalahari – safaris in northern Botswana
– Cry of the Kalahari – safari to Deception Valley and Okavango Delta, Botswana
– Livingstone's Footsteps – Chobe, Ngamiland and Okavango Delta, Botswana

Let's hope that some of these titles will stimulate sufficient interest for you to write off for a brochure – we have not met any other firm which can provide such a diverse and interesting range of tailor-made safari-type travel, though there are, of course, a number of travel groups that cover exploration in a similar way, but these are normally designed for people a little younger. One shouldn't be ageist, but mobility is a factor on such journeys.

• **Walking holidays** don't take one so far away, but the holidays in Europe organised by **Alternative Travel**, 67-71 Banbury Road,

Oxford OX2 6PE (01865 513333) are an absolute delight if you are fond of walking. One of the authors has been twice with them, and is planning to repeat the experience. The attractions are that each walk is well planned, generally in very beautiful country, the organisers take your luggage to the next stop while you are walking, you eat in local restaurants (with as much wine as you like included in the price), and there is generally a companionable group of 15 to 20 people to enjoy all this with. What more could one wish for? The main journeys include the following:

Italy

    Paths to Rome, to Orvieto, and to Urbino
- Tuscany and Southern Tuscan Trails
- Unknown Tuscany and Unknown Umbria
- Way to Assisi
- Sicily
- Sardinia
- Verona and the Dolomites

France
- Paths of Provence
- Cevennes
- Dordogne
- Basque Country

Spain
- Camino de Santiago
- Sierras of Catalonia
- Andalucia
- Sierras of Rioja
- Gateways to Aragon

Portugal
- Alto Minho and Alto Alentejo

The walking is none too demanding, and it is usually possible to return with the jeep that has brought the lunch en route if the morning has provided sufficient exercise. We cannot recommend these holidays too highly – as long as you really enjoy walking!

There are of course other walking tours available, particularly from the **Ramblers Association** via **Ramblers Holidays**, 13 Longcroft House, Fretherne Road, Box 43, Welwyn Garden City AL8 6PQ (01707 331133), who are well worth getting in touch with.

- **Cultural tours** of various kinds are a very popular activity for people who have sufficient time and money to feast themselves on treasures from the past, normally overseas. One of the best known organisations in this field is **Swan Hellenic**, 77 New Oxford Street, London WC1A 1PP (0171 800 2200); their cruises have the advantage of your being able to tour around different coastlines and call at a number of interesting sites or cities without changing your hotel. In addition there are guest lecturers and guides who have been selected because of their intimate knowledge of the subjects being viewed, so you have both the advantages of a cruise and the support of experts when visiting national treasures.

  There are other agencies who concentrate on such features as well, such as **Martin Randall Travel**, 10 Barley Mow Passage, London W4P 4PH (0181 742 3355), who specialise in small-group cultural tours to Europe and the Middle East, **Voyages Jules Verne**, 21 Dorset Square, London NW1 6QG (0171 723 5066), who arrange some fascinating tours all over the world, and the **National Art Collections Fund** who organise similar tours through **Specialtours**, 81A Elizabeth Street, London SW1W 9PG (0171 730 2297).

- **Cricketer Holidays**, 4 The White House, Beacon Road, Crowborough, East Sussex TN6 1BR (01892 664242) are worth a special mention. They have little to do with cricket any longer, though the organisation started by taking cricketers to Corfu and then developed by focusing on choosing places that were away from tourist areas. They have a style which we have found to be of great appeal; you can rely on a congenial group of people in a group, with locations and facilities that have been well researched by the principals, Ben and Belinda Brocklehurst. Formerly concentrating on Europe and the Middle East, they now include Madeira, The Gambia, St Kitts, Grenada, Barbados, Zimbabwe,

South Africa, Namibia, Sri Lanka, Malaysia, Sarawak, Sumatra and Penang. Their holidays represent sound value for money, and you can rely on better support than you would get with most package holidays.

Leisure

Leisure is the third feature in this category, and it is surprising how many people are in fact unable to relax and really enjoy a time of leisure. We have been challenged more than once during Future Perfect workshops about the need to develop active portfolios when there may be a strong desire to do virtually nothing for a period of time. It is about *being* rather than *doing*, and we have to agree that developing a capacity for relaxing and just 'being' can be enormously valuable. Not only does it provide an opportunity for genuine recreation, but it may be necessary at certain times in life to remove every possible stress and just have time for reflection, for reading and possibly walking, with an absence of demands from others.

More active leisure, by going to the theatre, opera, ballet, concerts and the like we also believe to be beneficial, being a necessary component in a balanced life and career portfolio at any age or stage. Many find it difficult to organise such activities, and time passes by without the stimulus of live entertainment – it is therefore a valuable opportunity if more time becomes available to make a particular effort to book up a series of shows or concerts. Season tickets at theatres or concerts series can be an excellent means of getting dates in diaries, which is normally the main problem. The advice we give, therefore, is not to neglect your leisure needs and to devise ways and means to spend time how best it suits you.

10. Do Something Outrageous

Although many people claim that they would like the chance to do something completely different, few of us seem to have the courage to actually achieve this in practice. If you look at someone's lifespan in its entirety, though, the only times when you are free from conventional demands are following higher education before you start your main career and then after you have left it (before becoming too decrepit). So why not throw caution to the winds and break out of your traditional mode? Some of our colleagues and acquaintances have done just this, quite a few as a result of participation in a Future Perfect workshop, and we describe below some of these initiatives or ventures to encourage consideration of similarly imaginative projects.

- **Peter and Brian** decided to sail the Atlantic as a challenging initiative in their Third Age. We understand that this was quite an adventure, the most eventful occurrence being a complete failure of their electrics just off Bermuda. Radio contact enabled them to cope, however, and the suggestion that one might be seized by terror in such a situation (e.g. from being run down by a larger vessel) was scornfully rejected. It was all in a day's sailing.

  Perhaps you might like to consider something similar? One couple on a Future Perfect workshop decided there and then that they would sell up and move to a suitable house that would be close to the sea or a river to enable the husband to sail and be large enough for the wife to have a studio. This seemed fairly outrageous to them, though not quite as adventurous as sailing the Atlantic.

- We have a colleague, **Mike**, who took a year off before committing himself to a Third Age career and single-mindedly sailed to the Aegean and elsewhere en route to enjoy a totally different lifestyle – he has never regretted it, and, if the truth be known, we suspect that he was sorely tempted to adopt that way of life permanently. It was evidently an important milestone in his life, and he will frequently refer to the time 'when I got off the boat....'. Sailing around the Greek Islands for a year is therefore an option you might like to consider!

- **John and Marianne** seemed to tire of their relatively tranquil life in a beautiful house in the Gloucestershire countryside. John is a management consultant who branched out on his own in his 40s, working from home so that he could see more of his family – but the two daughters grew up and left home for university. So John and Marianne bought an old Dutch barge – a converted 50-ton Dutch Baksuit barge, iron-built, 1925, powered by a 52hp marine diesel – and refurbished it themselves to become a travelling other home and mini conference centre, based in St Jean de Losne, France, and plying the French rivers and canals as the fancy takes them. We have seen photos of the barge after refurbishment and can see why it is rarely possible to contact them any longer in the UK – it really looks delightful, with a surprising amount of space. This has been a highly successful venture, and we congratulate John and Marianne on their persistence in bringing a pipe dream into a reality and carrying it through to such a magnificent outcome. You should visit them and see for yourself!

- **Paul and Carole** had lived in the same locality for the whole of their lives, with the majority of their relatives and friends living also in the same area. When Paul left one of the major banks to start his Third Age, he and Carole decided that they had to break out of this stifling mould and do something outrageous. So they considered moving house to somewhere quite far away, in the country. This idea was confirmed when Carole noticed a particular house in a magazine on a Christmas plane journey to Switzerland. 'That's the house we must have,' she declared. Believe it or not, this is the house they ultimately bought, after about a year's negotiation. It is an Italianate Rectory, built about 1850, with a very distinctive architectural style and is an extremely attractive building, both inside and out. To their chagrin, however, the house required virtually a new roof and a rebuilt chimney stack before it was really habitable. This has all seemed worthwhile, though, and the highpoint came when their daughter was married from the house; the fairy-tale wedding, with a large marquee in the one-acre garden and the illuminated facade, was a startlingly successful event and set the seal on their courageous venture.

- **Peter** was a lifelong and successful business consultant, who had an underlying wish to do something completely different – ever since, it seemed, the time when he was made redundant for a spell and had then to consider the complete range of options available to him. Finally, when sufficient funds had been accumulated, he decided to leave his firm in his mid-50s and start out as a wood-work apprentice on a two-year course at Parnham, where, incidentally, Viscount Linley had also learned the craft of making beautiful furniture. This desire had been stimulated by a successful visit to Wiston Project School in South Wales, mentioned earlier, with his partner, and they both came away with exquisite pieces of furniture that they had made during their stay there. If this isn't outrageous then we don't know what is – Peter has had to move during term-time to live in rented accommodation on the South Coast, is earning no money, with a partner and a house in Central London. We understand that the ultimate intention, though only embryonic at this stage, is to make furniture commercially, based on this cathartic experience – so watch this space! It is interesting that many people in their Third Age seem to feel that their practical, physical, sensual and craft faculties have been badly neglected and underexercised, and see a golden opportunity to do something about it.

- **Tony and Marion** are full of energy and can frequently be seen jogging around the streets at any hour of the day or night. He is a doctor, aged 60 plus, she a nurse, so they are practising what they preach and are determined to maintain a high level of fitness. Some years ago they decided to augment their fitness programme by taking up cycling seriously, believing that there are considerable medical benefits. 'It strengthens the heart, reduces stress, lowers blood pressure and builds stamina,' claims Tony. They now cycle regularly and participate in such major cycling events as London Zoo's 55-mile Life Cycle from Regents Park to Rochford in Essex. They also rove on their bikes on holiday and have been to Ireland, Cuba, Norway, the Pyrenees and New England in the US. In 1995 they took an adventurous European holiday and joined a demanding cycling programme starting in Prague and ending up in Venice – they claimed that it was a very relaxed holiday! We are afraid that just writing about such energetic endeavours makes the authors feel weak at the knees.

Partner support seems to be a key element in many of these outrageous – and perhaps some not so outrageous – ventures. For a major venture to be successful the active support of a partner would appear to be absolutely essential. We suggest that the relationship could be described as consisting of two pillars, each separate in their togetherness but together in their separateness. The whole purpose of the relationship, therefore, is for partners to allow, encourage and stimulate each other to do something outrageous for themselves. This may mean that they do it together – e.g. when buying a boat or moving house – but it may equally mean that one partner branches on his or her own, possibly at some cost to the other partner. This may well represent a new phase in the relationship, requiring some sacrifices to be made, but attaining a goal of personal fulfilment – the achievement of some deep longing – makes it ultimately a uniquely rewarding experience.

These remarks assume that you actually have a partner, and we appreciate that this will not be the case for every reader. You may be single, widowed or separated – or perhaps thinking about becoming separated because living together at such close quarters is just not working out. This is surely the time when a reappraisal is necessary if you are in any of these categories. You could live for another 20 to 30 years and should therefore try to consider as objectively as possible whether you would like to share those years with someone else or not. There will be many who will revel in the freedom of being single, but there are others who will have an underlying desire to live with someone else, not necessarily in a sexual relationship but a companionable one. So why not experiment? It is beyond the scope of this book to recommend ways and means of so doing, but we suggest that a clear personal analysis is the first and essential step to a potential new journey in life and relationships.

9

Making The Right Choices

You should by now have a sound knowledge of the two fundamental components that are necessary for a productive planning process to take place:

- A definitive statement of your **aim in life**, supported by an **inventory of your personal strengths, skills, and other relevant qualities**.

- An understanding from the previous chapter of the **life and career opportunities** which are available to you at this stage in your life.

It would be quite understandable, though, if your mind were in a whirl and you were unable to sift through the thoughts that you had been mulling over while you considered all the activities mentioned. Most of us would genuinely like to start out on ten times the number of initiatives that we could comfortably handle – which is why planning is so very important. The way we have found it advantageous to deal with this situation is to let your thoughts run riot and write down *everything* that you would ideally like to do before you reach your Fourth Age of dependency and decline!

So in the spaces below please list all the activities, great or small, that you would like to initiate (a) in your career and (b) in other areas of your life – have a real brainstorming session with yourself and get it all down on paper, however stupid it might seem at first.

Just write down every idea that comes into your head within the context of 'I want....':

(a) In your career

e.g. set up a home office, work as a consultant from home

....

....

....

....

....

....

....

....

....

....

....

....

....

....

....

....

....

....

....

....

....

....

....

....

....

....

....

....

....

(b) In other areas of your life

e.g. travel to India and the Far East, build a workshop

....
....
....
....
....
....
....
....
....
....
....
....
....
....
....
....
....
....
....
....
....
....
....
....
....
....
....
....
....
....
....

Before you consider any of these 'wants' further, you should be aware that you may convince yourself that none of the 'wants' are really feasible and that it would be much better to adopt a low profile and do almost nothing. We call this enemy lurking in your subconscious your 'Monkey on the shoulder'. When, for example, you think that it might be a good idea to join a local dramatic group your monkey might pop up and say, 'What, you join a dramatic group? But you can't act! They'll all be much better than you and you could look really foolish. What on earth would the family think of you – how embarrassed they would be.' And so on. The monkey has destroyed your self-confidence before you have even started to think about the possibility in more depth – if you let it, that is! The secret is to be aware of this particular danger, which affects absolutely everyone, and work through a logical process to neutralise the effects of the monkey on the shoulder and then arrive at a realistic assessment of the suitability of achieving a given 'want' on your list. How is this done? Well it works like this:

Supposing the monkey says, for example, that you are too old to

– change your ways
– take a degree
– set up in business on your own
– learn a new skill
– move house
– start a completely different second career.

...you will have to ask *why* the monkey has thought this to be the case, and take yourself through the following three steps in response to this very valid question.

1. Check out the <u>reality</u>

• Is your current state of health, those aches and pains, a genuine constraint for that activity?

• If there is a query, get checked out medically and find out for certain whether or not that is the case.

- Depending on the outcome, define areas from which your health will exclude you, e.g. ballet dancing.

- Is this therefore an excuse rather than a genuine reason? Or are you just lazy?

2. Review your perceptions

- Is it *your* personal assessment or have you taken over attitudes expressed by parents years ago that are no longer relevant? It often happens.

- By talking to a friend you might be able to highlight the real issues – might it be that a lack of confidence is the main obstacle?

- Possibly counselling could be beneficial, to give a wider perspective and understanding.

- If new areas tend to frighten you, why not talk to others with directly relevant experience, e.g. those who have taken a degree or moved house recently, to find out what it has been like for them.

3. Consider past difficulties overcome by self and others.

- Remember past daunting events when you overcame difficulties; you probably didn't imagine that you would ever make it then! What about going to a new school or taking impossibly difficult exams?

- Consider other models and examples, such as a lady getting an MSc at 83.

- If you were able to set intermediate goals it could make the whole task seem so much more achievable, e.g. you could allow yourself the option of dropping out of a degree course after one year if it didn't work out as you had anticipated – and this break-point could apply to virtually any activity. The advantage of the Third

Age should be that you are beholden to no one but yourself, though financial imperatives may drive you in the short term.

The 'monkey on the shoulder' is a very real phenomenon, which is why we have emphasised its insidious nature and suggested a means of getting rid of it. If you have problems in this area it can be helpful to draw up what we term an 'affirmation statement'. For example, you might write down, after due consideration:

> 'I am a skilled and experienced professional in the field of engineering design, with a potential capability to earn substantial fees in a consultancy role in the years to come, building on my network of business contacts and proven interpersonal strengths.'

Such a statement can then be put on a yellow sticker above your desk at home and, if possible, memorised and/or repeated regularly to reinforce your determination to make a success of a completely new way of working. This may appear bizarre at first, but one of the authors has done just this at a time of transition and has found it to be of significant benefit. We all need to boost our self-confidence when we are facing entirely new scenarios, and there is absolutely nothing to be ashamed of in taking whatever steps are necessary to address this situation. We are convinced that it is what is in our mind – i.e. the strength of our will to achieve something – that is the single most important factor when deciding to take up a new activity if we are to be successful. A half-hearted approach is almost guaranteed to fail.

It might be encouraging for you to consider the positive aspects of ageism if you are worried about being older, since older people:

- do have more experience
- can have more patience
- often have more developed social skills
- can be more tolerant
- are generally more open-minded (because they have less to lose)
- are self-confident and less apprehensive
- can calm troubled waters
- distinguish between results and activity

- are happy to work part-time
- will do jobs that younger people see as 'dead ends'
- have got 'youthful enthusiasms' out of their system
- are prepared to say what they think
- know who they are, and what they are capable of (and what not)
- think more about the team, less about themselves
- can be free of mortgages and onerous family commitments
- are 'laid back' and less 'hung up'
- can handle detail and are more accurate
- think before they rush in
- are more aware of downside risks
- have seen it all before, are 'older and wiser' based on experience.

This list of attributes is taken from the Institute of Management's publication (1989) *Too Old at 40?* and the findings of 'The Carnegie Inquiry into the Third Age' published in 1993 under Health (pp 7, 8) reinforce these positive qualities through their research. The Inquiry found that 'experience and expertise usually counteract any potential decline in cognitive function' and that older people can generally benefit from training and perform just as well as younger people, age not being a critical factor unless the tasks involved are physically demanding. It is therefore something of a myth that you are 'finished' at, say, 60, but many believe this to be the case because they have been told about the negative aspects so often. Our message to you is that you are as young as you feel, and that there is no evidence that your age will prevent you from carrying out the projects that you want to.

Options Mapping

But what *are* the projects that you would like to carry out? You should by now have drawn up a long list of 'wants' in the spaces provided above, and the next step is to try to determine which of those is immediately of greatest importance to you.

We suggest that you consider those which fall into the category of either Career or Family (usually the most significant targets) and star (*) the top three or four which you would like to tackle within the next few months or when you leave your main career job in future months or years. This is actually a critical assessment, because it will be likely to determine how you spend your life over the next few years – it could perhaps be excitingly different, if you so choose, or it could be much of the same, which, though comfortable, might be less fulfilling than a new venture of some kind.

The crucial aspect in choosing between options is to match your stated aspirations, your Aim in Life, with your personal qualities and what is realistically achievable. Business executives, for example, might be so brainwashed with the glamour of a successful business life that he decides to set up his own business, not realising that he had largely depended previously on being part of a competent organisational machine. Such a person may well not have the predominantly business qualities in his/her make-up, and would be wise to listen to his inner voice regarding his true inclinations and competence.

It is our view that people actually know what lies within, but often tend to deny any negative vibes – visible success at any cost, they will claim to be their aim. For many having a role in business is an alien activity; it is only because of the need to earn a living that they have ended up doing what they have been doing, often accidentally. So surely this is the opportunity to start spending time doing what you want to do, and your 'starred wants' should reflect your inner aspirations rather than your view of what convention (or your family) expects of you. We are sorry to labour the point, but we feel it to be vital.

Many will respond by claiming that 'it's all right for you, you have enough money to live on but I haven't'. Well, it depends how much it will cost you to live a basic existence and what you may wish to spend money on additionally. Surely it doesn't matter what the neighbours think if you don't take holidays or paint the house if you are doing what you really want to do, such as paying for a degree course while earning nothing and living off savings? It will be quite different for each person, but we do make a plea for radical thinking, uninfluenced by the anticipated views of family and friends! You should be aiming to live primarily for yourself at this stage in life.

Before we enter into further considerations of the options you are going to choose and to work on, we thought that it would be of interest to note the reactions of participants at the half-way stage of the first ever Future Perfect workshop held in the Hatton Court Hotel, Gloucestershire on September 8/9 in 1989. The main lessons learned by them were highlighted as follows:

- Concentrate on strengths
- Gifts and positive qualities have been identified
- I am *not* too old!
- Sharing thoughts is important
- Reasons for not doing things are usually excuses
- Find your real purpose in life – all flows from it
- You can achieve whatever you want if you make a commitment; no limits exist other than those that are self-imposed
- *We* can decide how we spend our time
- It is silly to say 'I haven't the confidence!'
- Be aware of the constructive use of time – plan your year
- I need some artistic outlet
- We have a lot of common needs/visions
- Everyone wanted to make a contribution (to helping people)
- I am my own enemy
- My visions/goals/objectives are changing
- I've got rid of the idea of retirement!

It was a diverse group of men and women, mainly in their 50s, and their reactions were succinctly expressed – not untypical of the reactions of anyone participating in this process, but markedly different, we suggest, from a conventional view of life after one's main career had ended.

Choosing the Key Options

We use two special sheets for setting out the main 'wants' that you have chosen (see Figures 9.2 and 9.3 on pages 190-193). The first is entitled 'Choice and Commitment. Its purpose is to enable a whole range of preferred options, covering every area of life, to be shown as intentions on a single sheet of paper. It becomes much easier, we have found, to get your mind around the development of a life and career plan if you are able to draw together the main components on one sheet. On the completed sheet in Figure 9.1, you will note that there are two groupings of commitment, the main ones being shown against **Family** or **Career/Activity**, which will represent the major projects to be developed and undertaken, with the secondary intentions in other areas of life shown under separate headings.

We have included some typical examples in Figure 9.1 so that you can appreciate the sorts of goals that you might wish to include in your plan. Let's examine each intention. The 'Choice and Commitment sheet' has been completed by Robert, who has a wife Jane, two grown-up children, John and Rosemary, each with their own family. Robert is planning what to do about his future life and career once he leaves his main career job in six months' time. His 'starred wants' are shown with key points highlighted on the sheet.

Project A: Set up gardening service

Robert took the view that he had had enough of a conventional office job and wanted to do something different. One activity he had always enjoyed, but rarely had the time for, was gardening. To his surprise, the more he thought about it the more he felt that that was what he really wanted to do. It would keep him fit, it would generate a bit of cash, he would be able to benefit from working in the open air and, to a degree, control the extent to which he worked on this activity.

He also had a friend, Ted, who was similarly inclined, and they thought that it would be ideal if they could combine forces and set up in business together; they would then be able to cover for each other for holidays and sickness and share the small amount of administration involved. Initially, however, he would have to discuss the proposition with Jane to ensure that it would not clash with any of her plans. Provided that she was in agreement, he would then have to approach the opportunity in a businesslike way and carry out some form of local market research. This might consist of looking at the competition, at appropriate methods of advertising and gaining referrals (via a local garden centre?), even knocking on doors to check out potential demand.

Figure 9.1 Choice and commitment — setting goals

Areas of life	Starred wants / SET UP GARDENING SERVICE	DEVOTE MORE TIME TO FAMILY	WORK FOR LOCAL CHARITY	TAKE UP EDUCATION COURSE
Family	• Check if OK with Jane	• Talk with Jane about possible new joint activities • Visit John, Rosemary more often • Look after children		
Career/Activities	• Research local market • Join up ewith Ted • Work out rates and distribute handbills • Start working!		• Investigate local needs • Draw up shortlist and meet people • Choose best route	• Examine possible courses • Review time and costs • Identify options and choose one • Get learning!
Appearance	• Go on a hip and thigh diet	• Buy some more imaginative clothes		
Help to others	• Visit old Phyllis regularly		See above	
Friends	• Invite group of friends for meal/game of cards once a month			
Fun/Activities/Culture	• Go to a show or jazz concert at least four times a year	• Tidy up workshop and make something	• Go on woodwork course	
Health	• Fix up walking holiday abroad	• Swim or play badminton once a week with Jane		
Home	• Decorate hall	• Put new floor in attic	• Get outside of house painted	
Money	• Review financial situation in more detail	• Get advice from Bert (Lloyds Bank)		
Spiritual	• Go to church more			

Together with Ted he would determine the most appropriate way of working, set fee rates that would be in line with the going rate in the area, and then draw up what would in effect be a business plan for the project. Assuming this were satisfactory he would design, print and distribute handbills advertising the service accordingly – and then start working! It would be very unlikely if he hadn't picked up one or two jobs during the research period, and should therefore be able to get the business off the ground relatively quickly.

Project B: Devote more time to family

This title has something of a hollow ring to it, considering just how many times executives or professionals who are also mothers or fathers have sworn to improve the situation at home during their main careers! Nevertheless, with a portfolio arrangement it should be possible to make up for lost time, to a degree, and cultivate the family you had not spent as much time with as you would ideally have wished. This is actually a project (and there are evident benefits in defining it as a project) which many people include as part of their future plans. Robert felt that the first priority was Jane, and he would aim to spend much more time with her and together they would work out some interesting activities that could be shared; perhaps a drawing or painting course, or some imaginative holidays that would previously have been impossible.

Then there were the children, John and Rosemary, with their own families. John lived some way away, which presented some difficulties, but Rosemary lived locally and Robert thought that he could make more efforts to help with the children by taking them out, babysitting and generally being more supportive than he had been in the past. Does that strike a chord with any reader?

Project C: Work for a local charity

Robert, like many others, felt that he wanted to give something back to society. The only problem was that he wasn't at all sure how to go about it, and had never before even considered getting involved in the voluntary sector (he had felt that it was full of wishy-washy do-gooders, which didn't really appeal, but he had second thoughts after talking further with one or two people in the know). So he decided to treat it like a business proposition and start by considering what the local needs might be, so that he could respond accordingly.

He did not feel competent to establish a charity himself, and wisely considered that supporting an organisation that existed already would be preferable. So he planned a visit to the public library to gain the basic information, and then to ask around to supplement the findings with the opinions of local people who were involved on the fringe of such activities, e.g. doctors, magistrates, social services, police, etc. From this activity he expected to arrive at a short list of organisations which he could then meet, and explore with them the possibility of his becoming a volunteer in a given field. He couldn't at this stage see where this might lead him, but it seemed to be a logical process to get things going and to enable his resolve to be turned into a realistic activity.

Once he had met people in their own work situations, following the detailed research, he felt that he would be able to make a much better assessment of the potential so far as his involvement was concerned. He saw it like a business proposition in which he would have to size up the organisation, assess the requirements and whether or not he could fulfil them (and/or wanted to!), and to consider just what he might get out of the involvement personally, since every activity represents a two-way situation.

Project D: Take up an education course

Robert realised that he would need to consider his previous satisfactions and declared aspirations in much greater detail, but he felt, from what he had gleaned from others, that it could be highly satisfying for him to enrol for an appropriate academic or practical education programme of some kind. He was somewhat academic by inclination, and therefore saw a minimum project as being a one-year part-time course – with a possibility of it lasting for three years.

The choice of subject, however, tended to throw him, and his thoughts were ranging from something related to his interest in gardening (e.g. botany, ecology, landscape gardening, plant life/protection), through to art history, painting and sculpture specialities, or even to technology subjects in which he had always taken a close interest – he was one of the first managers to insist that his team members should each have their own PC, and was fascinated by the potential of the Internet. He thought that the only way to resolve this situation was to examine the possible courses available to him so that he would gradually become aware which might be the most suitable for him. After all, his main objective was to find something that was satisfying in itself, rather than an opportunity to gain a diploma or degree for external recognition. Therefore the detailed arrangements – e.g. the reputation of the college, the particular venue, the frequency of attendance, the time and cost that would be involved – would all be vitally important features in arriving at the best conclusion.

So he aimed to select two or three options as a result of his explorations, and then choose one of them on the basis of a reasoned assessment, which would include a visit to the College and, if possible, a talk with the main Tutor involved. Enrolment would follow swiftly, he hoped, but he realised that this would normally take place only in September/October each year and not at any time in between.

The specific intentions under the other life and career headings are shown as indicated, and will be commented on briefly as follows:

Appearance
'Go on a Hip and Thigh diet' and 'Buy some more imaginative clothes' represent typical aspirations in such a plan. Most people seem to realise that you need to pay attention to your looks as you get older, and lifestyle and clothing are very significant contributors to a lively and attractive appearance. Putting it into practice may well require the active stimulation of a partner, though!

Help to others
Frequently the involvement with a specific charitable activity is the way that people cover this aspect, i.e. Project C would be the main outlet for this role in Robert's case. There is a huge general need,

however, as those with elderly relatives will appreciate, for lonely or housebound people to be visited on a regular basis. Hence Robert's intention to 'Visit old Phyllis regularly' demonstrates his concern for this increasingly common feature of modern life.

Friends

On some Future Perfect workshops we have asked participants to analyse their time allocation between main activities or people, and everyone is usually surprised by the very small amount of time (around 5%) given to meeting friends. This may not be significant in the short-term if both partners are working, since much social activity occurs informally at work, but if one is working from home or travelling around it is worthwhile considering how best to cultivate and retain good friends. Our view is that this needs working at, and that relevant activities need to be planned that will stimulate the ongoing development of a suitable circle of friends. Robert and Jane have therefore planned at least one event per month for inviting friends for a meal or a game of cards.

Fun/Activities/Culture

Again these need planning, in our view, and 'Go to a show or jazz concert at least four times a year', 'Tidy up workshop and make something', or 'Go on woodwork course' represent commendable objectives to ensure that this side of life is not neglected. If you are not able to allocate enough time to enjoy such activities at this stage in life, when will you ever?

Health

Most of us realise that maintenance of a good standard of health is a personal priority. Robert finds that walking is a relevant activity that he and Jane enjoy, so they are planning to 'Fix up walking holiday abroad' and, once a week, 'to swim or play badminton together'.

Home

This seems to us like a danger zone, where long lists are made out that are unlikely to be fulfilled – at least in the foreseeable future! So it is advisable to be selective, and Robert has cautiously planned to 'Decorate hall', 'Put new floor in attic' and 'Get outside of house painted'. Does this ring any bells with you?

Money

Here we strongly recommend the use of an appropriately qualified financial adviser, and we hope that 'Bert from Lloyds Bank' falls into that category and is not just a friend that happens to work there. We would go further, and suggest that you should select at least two financial advisers (if you haven't done so already), probably based on insurance policies taken out some years ago. In addition you might choose one of the leading insurance brokers, such as Sedgwick, Willis Coroon, Bowring or Bain Hogg. You will then be able to review your personal financial situation with them – the best practitioners require very accurate information and assessments – and make your conclusions by comparing the final outputs. It is evidently an opportune time to consider the potential implications of such aspects as inheritance tax, long-term care, and optimising the return on your investments.

Spiritual

As mentioned previously, people seem to become more interested in the spiritual side of life once they reach the age of 50 or thereabouts, and Robert's latent faith may receive a boost from his stated intention to 'Go to church more often'. We suggest, however, that there is much more to it than that, because it is possible to go to church regularly with only the vaguest intention of what it is all about. Conversely, there are people who never go to church but have a deep sense of spirituality and practice a loving, caring and wholesome approach to life that would put many so-called Christians to shame. So let's hope that Robert takes his intention seriously!

It is now up to you to follow suit and to use the blank forms indicated to set out your own detailed choices, to which you are gradually becoming committed. The second sheet, in Figure 9.3, can be used additionally to assist with exploring in greater depth the chosen short list of career or activity options – the starred 'wants'. This will be particularly relevant if a choice has to be made between conflicting projects, and should help to determine priorities for the ultimate decision-making process.

Figure 9.2 Choice and commitment — setting goals

Areas of life \ Starred wants		
Family		
Career/Activities		
Appearance		
Help to others		
Friends		
Fun/Activities/Culture		
Health		
Home		
Money		
Spiritual		

Figure 9.3 Development of career/activity options

	Career options	
	Option A:	Option B:
Tasks necessary to secure Option		
Positive features – PROs		
Negative features – CONs		
Impact on partner/ family		
Impact on financial situation		
Impact on quality of life/health		

Option C:	Option D:	Option E:

Achievement and Action – Drawing Up the Time Plan

We use a different form for concentrating on milestone targets and dates by which it would be reasonable to expect key actions to be completed. From Figure 9.4 you will see what Robert has determined would be appropriate for his main projects, and the time schedules are self-explanatory. Only he can really assess what is reasonable in each case, and he is intent on not making life too difficult by overburdening himself in the immediate future. He realises that the adjustment to this whole new set of activities and way of life will be demanding in itself, so he believes he is right to be cautious. We therefore suggest that you should follow suit and complete the blank 'Achievement and Action' sheet (Figure 9.5) so that you will have the basic tools for the subsequent phase – setting out on the new journey – covered by the next chapter.

Figure 9.4 Achievement and action – drawing up the plan

Time Span			
WITHIN 6 MONTHS	**WITHIN 1 YEAR**	**WITHIN 18 MONTHS**	**WITHIN 2 YEARS**
Research *2 months Business plan *3 months First client *4 months	Grow At least 10 clients *12 months	Grow At least 20 clients *18 months	Grow At least 30 clients *24 months
Review joint activities *1 month Start swimming or badminton *2 months Visit John or Rosemary *6 months	1 new activity by *12 months Have children to stay by *12 months Continue sport	Arrange walking holiday by *18 months Repeat other activities	
Research *2 months Shortlist *3 months Interviews *4months Start as volunteer *6 months	Start volunteer training and work as volunteer	Ongoing	Ongoing
Review possibilities *3 months Options selected *4 months Visit colleges and choose preferred option by *6 months	Register for chosen course by *12 months	Ongoing	Ongoing

Figure 9.5 Achievement ands action – drawing up the plan

	Time Span	
Starred wants:		

10

Comments By Research Participants On Choices Made

1. Operating Independently as a Self-Employed Contractor

- 'Easier for me than most because I went from being an employed management consultant to a self-employed one – and I knew the ropes about clients and consulting. Keeping costs down to a minimum meant that nearly all income was disposable – very important for peace of mind and keeping work level to a minimum.'

- 'It's a huge help having a profession – I am a chartered accountant – but you have to be prepared to work at a nuts and bolts level.'

- 'I manage very well. I don't work much – a day a week on average, if that. And my quality is much better as self-employed with low utilisation because I can take just as long as I want; I am under no pressure to finish in x days – no more and no less.'

- 'I only operate independently for a small amount of my teaching. I make more money when I work independently, but I have higher overheads as I have to buy equipment, books, etc. If my partner and I decide to work together we will have to be very organised and be particularly careful with the costing.'

- 'My original plan of one third NED, one third consultancy and one third charity is working well in all areas, but there is a constant need to network and weed out wasted non-income-producing time. It is often too easy to drift into loss-making work-in-progress – it is best to obtain cash up front wherever possible. Financially I am equal to or better than my previous main role; it is less political and I am providing more professional value to others. I also have a more flexible and tax-effective treatment of expenses than I had in my main role.'

- 'This applies to my role as a lay member of industrial tribunals. My long experience in management and industrial tribunals is being usefully employed, and the work is interesting and varied. It also applies to stimulating work I have carried out for two television companies as a historical researcher and as a management consultant for an embryo TV company.'

- 'The best prospect is always your previous employer, and I have been able to rely on admin support from the companies concerned. I have regarded this activity as extra money to be taken while available, though I have enjoyed it.'

2. Becoming a Specialist Consultant, Alone or With Others

- 'I am virtually a consultant, but, with one exception, I have never been paid. If your advice is worth seeking it is worth paying for.'

- 'Don't be afraid to ask for what you are worth. People will pay it, though the work may be sporadic. Right from the start ensure that you produce quality looking reports. Become part of a team with complementary experience; rarely will anyone want your knowledge in isolation.'

- 'I enjoyed working as a consultant in the first few years, but found I wanted to spend more time doing my own thing, e.g. writing.'

- 'I am one of a number of specialist consultants in the literary field, as one of a team of five. Much of the work is just that, but with enormous constraints through working within an education authority.'

- 'I work as a customs and tax adviser for the IMF, World Bank, UN, RIPA, ODA, etc. I have been surprised just how much work there is, and have frequently had to turn down assignments because of overlap on my time. It has been difficult thinking commercially – selling oneself – and doing the back-up administration, but it is good to be in a position of influence again. However, I find that I can gradually ease up on my assignments and have considerable control over how much I work; I like that.'

- 'It works very well for me (I am not financially dependent on my earnings). I have learned much about being my own secretary, business manager, etc. I enjoy the freedom to choose what I take on, and am also very conscious of ethical responsibilities and the need for careful attention to these.'

- 'This probably best describes my work for the museum – albeit unpaid! I find it very satisfying to be able to help members of the public with their queries, carry out research for authors, exercise a managerial role over my working party and its budget, and advise the Director of the museum on policy matters.'

- 'Work has been obtained principally through old colleagues, in most cases running their own business or after a move to a smaller company. Repeat business has nearly always resulted, meaning that I had to do no selling. It has worked out better than I would have thought possible.'

- 'Currently I am advising a PLC in some difficulties, and this arose from a proactive approach I made to its Chairman. The contract may lead to an invitation to join the Board (it did). Two assignments to date have arisen from professional contacts and personal networking; leading a consultancy project in Trinidad has been immensely stimulating, and acting as an expert witness in a banking/insurance fraud case was highly informative.'

- 'As a business and enterprise counsellor this has gone remarkably well, since the advice I give is based on experience of having done it actually myself, as in my last few years I was responsible for a group of small companies within the Group.'

- 'This has been interesting – I've gone to the other side! I am using the specialist knowledge and experience I gained in my last assignment (a secondment). I can choose which project I want to work on and therefore the amount of time I want to devote to it; the money is not important.'

- 'I haven't tried working with others and probably won't, because I don't want to build up chains of dependence which might become irksome.'

- 'In this work I am utilising my previous experience and adding to it. It has been necessary to adapt to different systems of work in development countries and sometimes necessary to suppress the remark. But we did it this way in the UK. In other words one's experience has always to be adapted to new and changing environments.'

- 'The assumption that I would network with others did not come to pass because I preferred the flexibility and independence of control (through working on my own) – but the downside has been some lack of stimulus in bashing ideas around.'

- 'I work on a lone basis. Marketing is a significant issue; it is essential to keep the networks going, such as dinner clubs, to keep people aware of what I am looking for.'

3. Fulfilling the Role of a Non-Executive Director

- 'This is more demanding and exposed than ever before – it is not a role for an amateur. How will you add value? Be prepared to give it quite a bit of time – these days much more is involved than attending a monthly Board meeting. If you have had a career in executive management remember that being non-executive is quite different! Don't take on too many.'

- 'It is not a sinecure. There can be a high expectation of a non-exec from employees. Time therefore needs to be allocated for getting around and understanding the business.'

- 'I have enjoyed my one non-exec job immensely because it is a congenial company/Board and it gives a sense of continuity and 'belonging' which you cannot/should not achieve in consultancy. I would like more non-exec positions.'

- 'First, don't expect a rush of headhunters and venture capitalists wanting your services; approaches take time to come. Second, don't accept the first one(s) that come along; be choosy and check them out thoroughly. When appointed, do your homework; pick your issues; get to know the other directors and turn up at meetings.'

- 'While I give valuable insight to the company through being at arm's length the role gives me a continuing and satisfying perspective on the financial services industry.'

- 'Most NEDs are not properly trained or appreciate their duties and responsibilities (under Cadbury *et al.*). The role of NED in public and private companies is gaining support, but is in some cases poorly paid – e.g. £500 or less per day; must attempt £1250/£1500 per day and keep proper records as to whether you achieve the desired figure.'

- 'Immensely enjoyable after being so many years an executive. I find that I can influence so many more situations, but it is hard to resist the natural inclination to get too involved and disempower the executives.'

4. Starting Up a New Manufacturing or Service Business With Others

- 'I would caution on this. By all means take a share stake, but try not to put up more than £10-£15,000 and certainly give no personal guarantees.'

- 'Anxious – but a lot of fun. I am lucky not to need an immediate income.'

- 'I would be chary of this because of the financial risk; I must necessarily be very conservative financially.'

- 'Choose the team carefully. Staff with quality people who should be able to grow the business. The culture of a small business is very different from most large organisations – the responsibility for people and business success is very real and direct; it's no longer Monopoly money.'

5. Working for the Community or for a Charity

- 'Always remember that voluntary organisations are not like commercial businesses. Everything takes longer; people of modest abilities may be doing stretching work; people get upset very easily. Only do it if you are really committed to the aims of the organisation and be prepared for a good deal of frustration. These observations are probably more germane to local bodies – some national charities are structured and run more like businesses.'

- 'You must be prepared to give a lot of time to the employees/volunteers, and must feel a real (com)passion and commitment to the cause. Patience is required with campaigners and users of services. It's not just a filler of time – others rely on you and you must put in the same work commitment as for paid work to succeed and give/receive fulfilment.'

- 'I have two trusteeships, and prefer to help strategically rather than in actual hands-on charitable work; also public policy involvement.'

- 'It's very hard to restrict the time and to make sure that you do only useful work. It's very easy to end up doing everything, especially if the others around you are less experienced or less well equipped. Charity committees can be appalling and talk all evening about quite unimportant issues!'

- 'I enjoy my chosen charitable activities – painting/sailing. I am uplifted by what I see of (a) the spirit in the youngsters I encounter and (b) the indomitable spirit of the terminally ill.'

- 'I've worked for the Shaw Trust for a couple of years. They are always very grateful – too grateful, I tell them, and explain what I get out of the relationship, e.g. the opportunity to test out new techniques and new training courses in a non-threatening environment. This is a real quid pro quo, not something invented by me to make them feel good. Also, I would expect them to give me a reference for good work.'

- 'I enjoy these activities; you get a sense of achievement/worth from them and you meet interesting people. In addition I help the London Philharmonic Orchestra – I am very fond of music and have been a listener/concert attendee for a long time. It has been fascinating to see behind the scenes of the orchestra and to be able to use my skills to help them develop their strategy, and to assist with their outreach work in education and the community.'

- 'There is so much to do – you must discipline yourself or else you would have no free time to enjoy life.'

- 'I drive for a caring charity, which works out very well. I give my time doing woodwork for another charity as they require it – it isn't demanding, but I believe that it's useful.'

- 'I thoroughly enjoy teaching French voluntarily in our local primary school. As I am not paid I can teach what I wish and can miss the occasional lesson without feeling too guilty! I find being a school governor interesting, but it is becoming an increasingly demanding unpaid job, both in terms of responsibility and time. I enjoy meeting the old people when doing Meals on Wheels and other members of the village when involved in local events. It is always fun doing things with other people, and it is important to be part of one's own community.'

- 'The problem is finding time to go to the meetings (often evenings) and the relative lack of organisation (compared to one's place of work).'

- 'Most rewarding, but hard work and frustrating at times.'

- 'As Chairman of the local CAB I have been able to involve myself to a far greater extent following the end of full-time employment.'

- 'Charities are becoming more like businesses in terms of disciplines and risks, as well as regulations and the need for tight financial discipline. Being a trustee is more like being an NED in terms of responsibilities. Can be very demanding dealing with technically driven non-financial people who are often out of touch with business life in the 90s. I am also chairman of a golf club where I led a management buy-out from the company which owned it for £3m. *Very* time consuming, and often having to deal with unreasonable members of the public. But if successful can be very rewarding in a non-financial sense.'

- 'I work for Abbeyfield, a charity providing accommodation for the aged, and it enables me to utilise my managerial experience as well as to help provide a worthwhile community service.'

- 'Worthwhile, though sometimes committees can be laborious! But development and pioneering with others in a new field to set up a National Register of Counsellors has been challenging, exciting, and often daunting in view of the multitude of issues involved.'

- 'I joined the local National Trust Association as a member, found that I was quickly put on the committee and, because of external events, became chairman within six months! It is enjoyable, I have met new people from all walks of life and so far it is a success. I enjoy activating the committee and they respond in good humour. I am meeting Princess Alexandra next week and we are planting trees, etc. All very satisfying, because none of us gets paid – money is not a problem for me (but I realise it can be for some).'

- 'I enjoy helping to run the local Community Association, which also provides me with needed social interaction.'

- 'Do only as much as you genuinely have time for and say *no* to all else. Think again if you do not find it rewarding, for it is only when you are enjoying it that you will do a good job.'

- 'As soon as you get involved in your chosen area, the demands on your time grow and grow. The organisations are invariably under-resourced and desperately need managerial help/experience. I suggest getting involved in only one or two and become deeply involved for greatest satisfaction (rather than many superficially).'

- 'There are plenty of opportunities to contribute to one's own professional area, to management organisations, and to the educational field – e.g. as a governor.'

6. Some Interesting Comments from Someone Who Has Chosen to Become a Full-Time Art Student:

- 'I cannot begin to tell you how good it feels to be alive for the first time in many, many years. I cannot really explain how, as a woman of 54, to be on my own, not having to work for money or be in the role of carer or professional specialist, is such a relief. To have time for just me alone, unfettered at last from domesticity and professional identity and obligation and competition is bliss. Personal freedom such as this comes at a price, but I was determined not to die full of resentment and the sense that I had only achieved for others at the expense of my own needs. There must be others who are perceived as high-achievers by their contemporaries, families and friends, but who nevertheless like me experience an internal void and lack of identity outside of role.'

11

Setting Out On A New Journey

This new journey is one over which you will be likely to have more control – welcome or unwelcome, as it may be – than you have experienced ever before. You will have made some initial choices about the tasks and projects that you intend to follow through, and will be wondering how you will be able to cope with the change to becoming your own boss. Having relied previously on a firm or employer to set down the overall guidelines for your working life, your new existence will be characterised by *freedom* and *flexibility* we suggest. This view is reinforced by one of the authors penning these words during a one-week break in Calangute, Goa: on his own, in February, immersed in sizzling heat and enjoying an enchanting Indian experience in a colonial-type hotel at very low cost. Such an initiative, regrettably, would have been virtually impossible during the majority of main careers.

A colleague tells us that he has now changed his priorities completely, though still very active in business mainly in South Africa. He takes his diary for the following year and first marks in the personal holiday and travel intentions for him and his wife together with their major social engagements; only then will he be prepared to consider taking on business commitments so long as they can be accommodated around those dates. It may sound somewhat extreme but satisfaction comes from *what you want to do*, not what convention tells you.

We therefore need to learn to listen to ourselves better if we are to enjoy our Third Age experience to the full. Just take the Goa trip as an example. The following are some examples of the comments offered before the trip commenced:

– 'How strange to go just on one's own.'
– 'You'll get amoebic dysentery going to India and will be ill for at least three months afterwards.'
– 'How will you manage completely on your own?'
– 'I hope you'll take good binding pills.'
– 'Do be careful.'

Yet visiting India had been a lifelong dream, and here it was, the dream actually being fulfilled. An unexpected by-product has been an improved understanding and appreciation of the content of Salman Rushdie's novels!

So what about you? You will have the best intentions of doing what you said you would, but will you actually do it? This aspect is discussed at great length on Future Perfect programmes; most participants realise that the hype of the workshop will no longer be with them a few weeks after the event, and that their enthusiasm may wax and wane during this time. It is for this reason we recommend that a formal follow-up session is arranged some 6 to 10 weeks ahead, when implementation of the life and career plans should be well under way, either one-to-one or with the group. This is, of course, not always possible, but there are a number of alternative measures which we strongly recommend should be put in place if you are at all serious about carrying out your plans. These include the following:

Arrange regular one-to-one sessions with your partner or a sympathetic friend.

This is probably the most beneficial recommendation based on personal experience and the positive feedback from others. The essential components are:

• Have your complete Life and Career Planning folder with you when you meet.
• Fix meeting dates in the diary well ahead, every one or two weeks

initially so you can ensure that the sessions take place (Sunday evening appears to be a good time for many people before the next week begins).

- Each session should last for one to one and a half hours, no longer.
- Review progress when you meet, project by project, and highlight priorities for the following period.
- Challenge or allow to be challenged every contentious aspect where progress appears to be lacking and dissatisfaction is expressed.
- Examine possible alternatives, both with regard to detailed project aspects and to changes in or variations of the original options chosen (as further data becomes available).

Many of us would recognise this as a 'supervision' session, which does not imply a hierarchical approach on the part of the 'supervisor', but a focus on the thinking, feelings and activities of the second person – the 'supervisee'.

We would expect marital partners to be able to carry out this task for each other with little difficulty though an unselfish attitude is necessary to allow a partner to express their independence! There are considerable potential benefits if the experience can be shared in this way since each partner's plan is likely to impact greatly on that of the other and appropriate adjustments may therefore be made during the sessions as the reviews progress.

Ask a supportive friend to phone you at regular intervals

This is to see how you are getting on. This would be additional to the above, from someone who is reasonably detached and is able to take an objective view of how you are going about things. It would naturally be helpful if you were to choose someone for this role who would be sympathetic to your aims and would understand the potential difficulties in carrying out some of the tasks, such as researching and selecting a favoured charity.

Make your intentions visible

This would include a whole variety of actions such as:

- Posting up a version of your timeplan on a wall near your desk at home or possibly in the kitchen; it should show clearly relevant milestone targets and key plan dates.
- Using coloured sticker notes for yourself in prominent positions and places regarding specific actions to be taken.
- Posting a few challenging notes, e.g. in the loo, asking 'How is the plan going?

This may seem daft but it often works. We all need reminding, but not too often.

One colleague confessed that he had put a sticker note on the door leading to the cellar instructing himself to 'clear out the cellar', to which he had become accustomed and had not yet responded (we will not comment on the extent of the elapsed time involved).

Foster or join a suitable network of fellow professionals

We have referred previously to the isolation that people can experience when cut off from their main careers, their colleagues, suppliers, customers and business contacts associated with them. There are two main options:

- Maintain membership of formal networks that you are already committed to at present. A former personnel director gave a typical personal example through retaining his links with Devonshire House, a relevant professional grouping.

- Seek out new networks of which you were previously unaware. Regrettably, it may be only by chance that you come across some of these linkages, which are frequently informal in nature. Any opportunity you come across should be seized with alacrity, we suggest; you can always withdraw if there doesn't appear to be a reasonable pay-off. We illustrate this feature by quoting three examples which have come to our attention:

–   **The Chartered Accountants Network**, initiated by the Thames Valley Society of Chartered Accountants. This is an enterprising venture for chartered accountants who are seeking permanent contract, interim or temporary employment, full or part-time. They regularly publish a very presentable list of qualified accountants, each with a comprehensive personal profile, from which prospective employers are able to draw. Should anyone be interested in this opportunity the telephone number is 01628-34146.

–   **The Success Group** describes itself as 'A network for creative sharing of work opportunities to benefit individuals and the community'. Based on regular dining club evenings, it provides a forum for discussing issues of common concern, focusing on a chosen topic on each occasion. It therefore aims to combine business and social aspects. If any reader is interested the telephone number of the co-ordinator is 01491-573148.

–   **The Network of Unlimited Skills (NOUS)** was launched with a great fanfare on 5 May 1995 at Brooklands, the theme being 'Let's put experience back to work'. This initiative was linked to and encouraged by the Association of Independent Computer Specialists (telephone 01494- 525707). The venture suggests using the IT highway, the Internet, to market personal skills and experience and offers assistance to bring this about (telephone 0181-942 4831). Community Whisper Groups are being set up in many towns and countries through the UK to further this network in a practical way.

These three examples of new networks and new initiatives highlight a longing for people who are like-minded to get together on a regular basis to share experiences. You may well say initially, 'That is only for wimps who lack self-confidence', but we would advise against such a hasty assessment.

We suggest from the feedback we get that everyone has a need to be a member of some grouping that is associated with their aspirations. This could be related to business (e.g. The Institute of Directors); to consultancy (The Institute of Management Consultants), to engineering or IT (various professional institutes) through to fine art and design (NADFAS) or religion (e.g. The Society of Saint Francis).

We are convinced that there are as many opportunities as one might wish for but why not start up something yourself if there is a niche that is not being filled? Perhaps our friend Robert, for example, could initiate a local jobbing gardeners' group to share experiences on favoured suppliers, to compare rates and to consider shared marketing?

Local community centres are the natural focus for such groups and we believe that such supportive action is beneficial to all parties involved. Local authorities would do well to sponsor more of this type of activity. A common need is marketing access and a relevant local initiative could benefit this aspect considerably.

So you should be well on the way to fulfilling the ambitions set out originally – to design, live and manage a balanced portfolio. It is possibly worthwhile to comment a little further on achieving a balanced portfolio in practice, since it is no easy task. We suggest that, as a practical guide, you might watch for the following danger signals:

- When your partner says, **'Is it always going to be like this?'** In other words he or she is implying that the situation is unsatisfactory and that at least one part of the portfolio is out of balance! Workaholic tendencies seem to persist well into the Third Age.

- **'I thought Wednesdays were to be just for us'** is another warning signal. A commitment has obviously been entered into which has not been consistently fulfilled.

- **'I'm sorry, I have to change our arrangements'**, if it happens too frequently, is a warning that is unacceptable in certain circumstances, particularly regarding important business engagements. It just highlights the fact that you cannot organise your life adequately and that you probably have conflicting loyalties/priorities – or just too demanding a portfolio to cope with.

- **'Are you still interested in us?'** is a sign that you have neglected some person or organisation that has been expecting you to be more involved than has turned out to be the case in practice. A genuinely proactive stance is normally required.

Managing in the Third Age is more often than not about learning to say 'no' when you are asked to do something (normally for free). We have met quite a number of people who bemoan the fact that they are working hard but getting paid nothing for it – yet it is their choice to do this. If you find yourself in this position it is perhaps helpful to question the desirability and the extent of your involvement in such an activity. The authors both understand the dilemma only too well and appreciate that saying 'no' is sometimes virtually impossible.

However, that must indicate a view on the part of the client that there is a need which you alone can satisfy – and you therefore have a difficult choice to make. Primarily we suggest you have to be true to yourself and if, say, an organisation is likely to collapse without you then it is possibly right that such fragility is brought to a head by your saying 'no' for a change. It would not be overstating the situation to repeat in one's mind 'You have the choice' when facing a dilemma of any kind but particularly when faced with taking on new commitments or new clients that will knowingly put you under great pressure. It is recognised that for many long-term illnesses 'pacing yourself' is a priority recommendation for minimising its effects; so too we believe to be the case with Third Age stress, and the resulting benefits if we pace ourselves accordingly. If you are able to arrange your commitments so that you feel entirely comfortable with the demands placed upon you then your life should be not only satisfying but healthy too.

Reflections on the Adjustment from a Main Career to a Third Age Lifestyle

If you haven't yet experienced such a transition it will probably be difficult to imagine the full impact that the change will make on you as a person, and on your partner and your family. The more superficial aspects are self-evident, such as having a little more freedom in terms of work patterns or taking a holiday when you want to, but the way you are likely to feel about things is not easy to determine. We have therefore gathered together relevant information from the Third Age research set up for this book, and discussed the most important issues with a number of the respondents.

One particularly thoughtful person, David, a former finance executive with a multinational corporation who moved on at age 50, took the trouble to highlight the specific issues he saw to be important.

His comments provide a very useful framework within which to highlight aspects of our broader findings:

Needing money

Money is not generally seen to be critical factor if a person moves on from their main career at age 50 plus, though it can, however, be or become a significant issue for those in their 40s. People aged 50 plus are normally approaching completion of their mortgage payments and financial commitments to children (unless there is a second family). This generation is therefore likely to be able to use the money they receive in a lump sum from their outstanding commitments and to live well above the poverty level on a partial pension, possibly combined with investment income from the proceeds of a parental home.

Our finance executive comments: 'I have been very lucky in not needing the money. It's not that we are well to do – and my pension doesn't start until I am 60 – but we don't spend a lot and there seems to be enough.'

We have found that Third Agers are frequently surprised that their expectations of becoming 'poor' just do not materialise; they tend to forget the savings made through opting out of a corporate lifestyle, and find that a more pragmatic approach to budgeting and expense yields a financially comfortable situation.

This cannot be said, however, for people in their 40s, who may well be saddled with significant liabilities in the shape of a mortgage with many years to run (possibly even with negative equity), children in the middle of their education, and little chance of inheriting any proceeds from their parental homes (because their parents are still living in them!). It consequently becomes absolutely critical for people in their 40s to find a source of income that will satisfy those needs in the coming years. Though this represents a considerable challenge to their resourcefulness, it can be seen as a positive feature in that the urgency of the need will be likely to drive the process described in this book to a point where a successful outcome is much more likely than for someone who doesn't need the money quite so much. In our experience this could be a blessing in disguise, since people change direction because of these constraints and emerge in due course with a life and career pattern which suits them well, and in which they can continue until they choose to wind down.

Many respondents in our research claim that they would have liked to have made the change earlier; the consensus is that around age 50 seems to provide a really positive opportunity to develop a new career pattern and associated lifestyle.

Staying healthy

Many of the people who come on our workshops rate 'staying healthy' as a very high priority. This is hardly surprising, since good health is an essential requirement if one is to be unconstrained in choosing and developing new life and career patterns in the Third Age. Yet for many this is barely an issue, since they have never experienced ill-health within their families, and their parents may still be alive or have died only in relatively advanced years.

The level of priority given to this aspect would therefore appear to correlate almost directly with the experience of serious illness and death in close family and friends. The authors have been touched and shocked by the loss of friends in their 50s or early 60s, and by the incidence of cancer – the latest example being one of a highly successful lady colleague who has been diagnosed recently as suffering from cancer of the bone marrow. In situations like this, the plans that have already been made and are in the process of being implemented need to be reviewed radically in the light of the changed circumstances.

However, many of us are of average health and probably do little to ensure that we take advantage of the wealth of good advice that is available to us – we are too fat, we eat and drink too much, and we take too little exercise. Perhaps the death of a close friend might prompt us into taking the issue of health in the Third Age a little more seriously. For there are some basic guidelines we can observe if we wish our bodies to keep up with our aspirations and intentions.

In Future Perfect we strongly believe that the life and career patterns that we establish have a disproportionate influence on our health. That is to say, from the psychological point of view, if we are highly motivated in how we are spending our lives the likelihood will be that our health remains at a high level. There will be no chance for apathy or depression to set in because of the adrenaline which pumps through the system as we tackle old and new projects with vigour and enthusiasm. A balanced work portfolio can provide just the sort of stimulus that is necessary, we believe, to maintain a healthy lifestyle – the main difficulty, of course, is to achieve the appropriate balance between a fulfilling workload on the one hand, and too much pressure and stress on the other hand caused by being over committed.

Interacting with the family

This is a fascinating issue which rarely, in our experience, comes to the surface. David, referred to earlier, says: 'The interaction with my family has been vital – though not always successful or easy. For all that I now know both my partner and my adult children, and they me, in a way that could never have happened had I continued in full-time work.'

I wonder if we can realise the extent of the power and the value that is contained in those comments, and the depth of advice implicit in the main theme taken up. Sadly, all too often children will say that they hardly know their father – and maybe their mother would be included as well in future years – so that there is a degree of catching up to be done which is well nigh impossible.

Similarly, many partners will claim justifiably that they have 'grown apart' over the years, and the Third Age move can then become the last straw which finally bursts the relationship apart. The partners of the authors are both psychotherapists, and we can two therefore comment by proxy on the basis of many examples fed to us (without breaching confidentiality) of the couples in this situation. There is one couple in particular where the husband had spent most of his main career visiting overseas customers and offices – home for a week or two and then another overseas tour – until he had to take early retirement. The resulting partner and family upsets have required extensive counselling in order to recapture and develop the slender threads of the original relationship when they chose to live together and bring up a family.

There is a dichotomy here, which is very mysterious. The Future Perfect research carried out by the British Market Research Bureau demonstrated that 48 per cent of the 217 respondents considered 'Family and personal relationships' as their most important life feature (with 31 per cent claiming 'Health' instead), and 77 per cent considered it to be in the top two features. But 'Work' and Money' accounted for only 6 per cent and 4 per cent respectively – so just what has gone wrong? People on Future Perfect life strategy workshops almost inevitably indicate that their family life is a high priority, and that is what they want to devote more time to. So why hasn't it been a consistently high priority during the main career period? Though it is difficult to generalise, a pertinent comment was made by our finance executive that 'Work is a great anaesthetic – like alcohol – and it's all too easy to use it to keep one's other issues at bay'.

We also see work as being addictive – like a drug – which powers the forces of self-esteem and peer recognition to the extent that the family is temporarily (and hopefully unintentionally) completely forgotten. This trend is becoming even more dangerous, we suggest, in the current two-tier society where the professional elite is working its socks off to maintain a competitive position. One of the authors was once told: 'If you can't manage your wife, you can't manage anything' – in other words, she must accept the demands placed on you by your firm if your career with them is not to be jeopardised.

The Third Age represents a wonderful opportunity to make up for some of those past omissions and to establish a much closer relationship with members of the family and old friends. Those who have managed to achieve this improved level of involvement testify to a great feeling of well-being – one research respondent quoted that 'I am happier now than I have ever been', and we know that his family life accounts for this perception more than anything else.

Needing to feel important

We mentioned above the peer pressures that are prevalent today regarding status, job title and position in a firm's hierarchy. People will sacrifice a great deal and work excessive hours to get that director title, and, once achieved, they cannot imagine ever being at any level less than where they have arrived at – despite the evidence to the contrary. But it can be rather like the situation when an MP ceases to be a Government Minister – his office, his staff, his car and possibly his house are taken away overnight, and the backbenches loom for the rest of the MP's career. Many find such a transition exceptionally difficult to take, and the higher one has risen the greater the fall, of course.

Most of us have never had exalted titles, but we have carved our niche and have a standing of kinds with colleagues, friends and neighbours. How are we going to feel about being just plain Alan or Kate to everyone? The conclusion we have reached is that the adjustment takes a considerable period of time – four years or so seems to be the consensus – and this is one of the aspects that gradually becomes less important. In fact, one of the authors works part-time for a charity, where one of the delights is that he is known simply by his first name and has no status other than that of being a volunteer. This has actually been a very positive experience, and has helped with the process of getting in touch with one's feelings and real identity.

David again comments that: 'It is much easier if one does not need to feel important. Much of the work I now do is quite menial and elementary, but I know it's useful and that I do it well. I observe that some of my former colleagues have difficulty in not being a chairman, director or whatever, and maybe some even fear that they won't quite know what to do if they are not in charge.'

We believe that this is a profound assessment, because many professional people operate within narrow boundaries and depend largely on others for their ultimate effectiveness. The world of organisational work, as seen from a Third Age standpoint, appears to be horribly constrained, full of grey-suited men and women living narrow, pressurised lives, beholden to their firms. Yet there is a much more liberated situation just round the corner, in which those self-imposed boundaries can be removed and life experienced more richly, taking advantage of new concepts and exploring new territories.

The move from 'Chief' to 'Elder'

Third Agers potentially possess qualities which are in very short supply in most walks of life. There are generally 'hidden agendas' for people in organisational life, whether it be in a firm, a hospital, a sports club – and personal ambition and self-aggrandisement is largely at the heart of it. For the mature Third Ager, however, those hidden agendas are mainly in the past and there is an opportunity to be more relaxed, more fair and objective in difficult situations, with the benefit of having experienced such difficulties before. This came home to one of the authors when assisting a charity with a particular project; a number of remarks were made to the effect that 'I feel safe with you involved', 'It's a great comfort to have you involved', etc. This was surprising to the recipient, but the reality appeared to be that they were looking on the person essentially as an 'Elder' – non-threatening, helpful and hopefully with a measure of wisdom from past life experiences.

In the authors' view this is a feature which should be recognised universally, so that a much more proactive stance may be taken by organisations to acquire or make a more enlightened use of these 'Elder' qualities. There are many relevant opportunities as mentors, advisers, governors, project leaders, and so on as indicated elsewhere in this book.

Personal growth

'In some way or other it's all about personal growth. I am not sure how, but I do think one's growth is at the heart of the whole thing. I am not sure how much it matters what I do all day, and whether it's socially productive or not. **'What is vital is how I feel about me at the end of the day',** comments David. I suppose it depends to a degree on how one defines or understands what growth consists of. In terms of Maslow's well-known hierarchy of needs, the apex of the pyramid is represented by 'self-actualisation' or 'fulfilment' – the final goal. Achieving real fulfilment, however, depends on knowing oneself to the extent of realising what will be ultimately fulfilling (beyond conventional life and career ambitions), which is why we place such emphasis on self-knowledge in this book.

It would perhaps be true to say that 'growth' at a mature age is an alien concept for traditionalists, such as those who announce very finally that they are 'retired' and simply that 'life' is now really over for them. Yet it is surely valuable to appreciate that growth – an increase in learning and understanding – can occur throughout mature lives, even, we are told, when dying of cancer in a hospice.

So how do you test out whether or not you are growing, and living a fulfilling life? We believe that David has put his finger on this by highlighting that the way one feels at the end of the day is what really matters – and actually being aware of those feelings. This does not mean to say that there won't be days when you feel lousy or a sense of despair, but that this will be counterbalanced by the many days when there is a feeling of contentment and an acknowledgement that you are spending time how you want to, and are enjoying it. Personal growth is surely occurring when this happens, as you become more the sort of person that you want to be as each day passes, looking inwards as well as outwards.

Francis Dewar, in his book *Live for a Change*, frequently refers to the 'Journey Inward, Journey Outward' pattern of life as an essential pattern for the development of wholeness, taking account of inner spiritual needs as well as outer physical needs. If you are really intent on personal growth you will have to pay attention to the whole person, we suggest, and this element should be included in the life and career plan that you draw upon reading this book.

12

Postscript:
The Future of Work

Responsibilities for Youth and New Opportunities for Elders in Post-Employment Communities of the Future

As we approach the millennium, the future of work is not what it used to be. A massive shift is already taking place; we as individuals must take responsibility for our own lives and livelihood in the post-careers society. Some commentators prophesy an end to work as we know it and predict a post-work society but there is no end to work in sight. We need it psychologically and economically. However, we are facing a post-employment society. In the past we looked to an employer, or the State, to determine our progress. In the future, the responsibility for providing will rest firmly on our own shoulders. Some form of life planning will become imperative for individuals, families and communities. Ideally this life planning should be from cradle to grave but more realistically it can take place at every age and stage of life. Western societies are now relinquishing the old Big Idea based on having tomorrow for a new Big Idea based on a new life and work paradigm, as described in Chapter 1. With the new Big Idea, individuals take satisfaction from being now, from living, working and relating creatively in the present, rather than waiting for something tomorrow which may never come.

The RSA (Royal Society for the Encouragement of Arts, Manufactures and Commerce) has launched a major project to help us move "Towards a New Definition of Work". In launching the RSA

Future of Work project, Sir Michael Heron, Chairman of the Post Office, who is the son of a postman and was formerly Personnel Director of Unilever, emphasised the importance of viewing *an occupation* as "activities which give individuals a role in life, a sense of purpose". Individuals now need to become self-reliant, not only economically but also becoming more psychologically resourceful within themselves. Sir Michael urged us to think of rewards as lucrative returns, and also to consider a broader and more balanced view of total rewards to include qualitative and psychological returns as well as economic ones. Barry Curnow also spoke at that launch about the implications of these changes for the individual. He outlined Future Perfect's experience in dealing with individuals and introduced the audience to the principles of *How to Live More than Once* in this changing world.

The RSA Future of Work project continues with an electronic debate on the Internet which is the first of its kind. At the time of writing this could be found at http://www.rsa.capgemini.co.uk .

According to a survey by Millward Brown International entitled "Powerful People", commissioned for *The Guardian* in the Autumn of 1996, 44 per cent of the respondents thought of changing their jobs at least once per week. "The overall impression is of a substantial core of workers who are both demoralised and demotivated". Some 70 per cent think of abandoning their career path at least once a month and a third of these once every day. Their preferences are for a complete change of lifestyle. More than 50 per cent intend to change employers within two years and nearly 30 per cent within the year, due to frustration with their current position rather than any particular career strategy. Nevertheless, despite uncertainty about the future which is an overriding concern, deteriorating employer-employee relationships, lower commitment and employee dissatisfaction with management (with over half citing bad management as a cause of stress), there are still signs of a remarkable resilience and robustness in how people cope with change. The survey identified six *personality types* characterising different responses to the changes taking place in the world of work: *Young guns* are mobile, overwhelmingly ambitious, thrive on change, work best under pressure and are unfulfilled. 20 per cent of them believe that contract work benefits both employer and employee. *Happy hard workers* are upbeat people who work long hours but get tremendous satisfaction from what they do. 65 per cent are totally committed, almost half are over forty and they are the highest paid group. *Underpaid/undervalued* are unhappy with pay and hours although both are better than average. They feel hard done by and should move on soon. Morale for them is at rock bottom. *Contented carers* represent 14 per cent of the sample, are satisfied with their pay, enjoy their jobs, have good work relationships enjoy slightly above average earnings, work the shortest hours and are often in the smallest organisations. 10 per cent are on short term contracts. *Professional moaners* are unwilling to try change because they think it's management's job to make things right. Many have plateaued in big organisations. 75 per cent male, 30 per cent of this group are stressed by fear of job loss. *Friendly team players* see people and teamwork as more important than long-term career prospects. They have less interest in adapting to new technology. 66 per cent are over 40, mostly women workers. Although they take pride in their work, dissatisfaction is increasing.

It is important to be flexible in our approach to the future. We do not know exactly what is going to happen but we can anticipate and prepare for the unexpected, as well as predicting alternative scenarios of what may happen. We can gear ourselves up appropriately. Information is one of the great planning tools to prepare for the unexpected. There seem to be three certainties in the foreground, against which to plan for uncertainties in the background:

1. We will no longer rely on the State to provide education, healthcare and pensions in later life;

2. We will have to constantly update our skills to remain marketable, in the face of technological change;

3. We can no longer rely on any job, occupation or career for life.

These three points must be considered together. We are expected to be increasingly responsible for our own life plans, career development and retirement. State pensions will be worth very little in future years and individuals must plan ahead and prepare to close the financial gap between income needs in retirement and what the state will provide. Individuals need to take charge and plan ahead for success in their lives and careers. There is too little financial planning for the longer and more expensive lives that we all face after our main careers stop, which is happening at a younger and younger age!

As ideas and technology change rapidly it will become common for people to enjoy (hopefully) or pursue (inevitably) three or four careers during their second and third ages. Some may naturally progress from one career or work module to another with a little overlap, while others will adopt a portfolio of careers which they pursue in parallel. Portfolio careers take much organisation and time planning and do not suit everyone. However, the results from skilful portfolio management of complementary projects can be spectacularly satisfying and successful.

Employers will prefer increasingly to employ a smaller core staff and to take on casual or temporary employees when and if they are needed. Therefore, most people will probably experience a period of self-employment, at some point in their working lives, either setting up a business of their own or working on a contract basis for one or more employers. This could seem nerve-racking for some, as short- term contracts appear to provide little conventional security either financially or psychologically. Yet fixed employment is a thing of the past in virtually all professions and careers. When no job enjoys a guarantee of longevity any more, what security is there in being employed?

Self-employment will often force an individual into life planning. If you run your own business then *you* decide how many hours you need to work, and *you* decide when to take a holiday... If self employment is approached in the right way it can provide the flexibility and freedom for a third age lifestyle that enables you to live 'more than once'.

By developing and experiencing the opportunities that the third age can offer, we can show the generations who follow how to maximise their skills and creativity and adapt to the continuous changes that they will face. At the same time, many young people today are insufficiently trained. Life planning is the key to understanding ourselves and our strengths. It is never too early to start even at school.

Third Agers will often find themselves in positions of advocacy for which their age and life experience will automatically position them as potential sources of wisdom: as consultant, counsellor, therapist, non-executive director or volunteer.

It would seem sensible, therefore, for third agers to use their influence in order to guide their younger colleagues into making life planning a habit. Of course, example is always more effective than exhortation and by living a full and satisfying life you will show others that change and transition can be positive and productive.

We now live longer than ever before and the majority of us will expect to be healthy and active well into our 80s. This means that some degree of life planning is essential if we are to make the most of our long lives and not give in to conventional retirement at 65. As the birth rate in Western Europe continues to fall, there will be a growing dependence on third agers to provide education, service and knowledge. The transition into third age will therefore become crucial to the development and progress of our communities.

Forces for Change

This book is a survival guide for handling the revolutionary changes taking place in our lives. There are ten separate, yet inter-linked revolutionary forces for change. Learning is essential precisely because we live in revolutionary times. We need to understand the rules of the new order. The management consultant or portfolio worker is affected by and must respond to the same revolutionary forces for change that affect clients. These forces provide much of the content of work with clients, helping them to manage change within their own organisations. They also form the context of the market environment in which the post career consultant or portfolio worker conceives and delivers his own services.

These ten revolutions, outlined below, have happened during the working careers of most individuals who are now in the second half of life and who have already seen the transformation of the workplace in an irreversible way. The changes are still taking place.

1. The Information Technology Revolution
2. The Communications Revolution
3. The Know-How Revolution
4. The Services Revolution
5. The Marketing Revolution

6. The Revolution in Labour Markets
7. The Careers Structures Revolution
8. The Revolution in Employee Expectations
9. The Revolution in Employer Requirements
10. The Pay Performance and Rewards Revolution.

The key features of the ten revolutions are summarised below.

The Ten Revolutions

1. Technology has driven the **Information Revolution**. The widespread availability of inexpensive computer power on an unprecedented scale has been made possible by the silicon microchip and its universal applications. This has dramatically altered the relationship between capital, technology and labour. Traditionally, human resources have been deployed since the industrial revolution in such a way as to reap maximum return from the other, scarcer factors of production: capital and machinery. The revolution in information technology has altered the balance of power between these factors, and has created changes leading to the nine other revolutions which, in turn, represent a strategic upheaval in major fields of the world economy. Information technology is now relatively plentiful, as is the money for projects that meet desired rates of return. This means that particular kinds of people and skills are now the scarce resource (rather than capital) to which technology and financial resources must be applied in the appropriate way. Of all the revolutions, information technology is seen as having the most positive effect on an organisation – although men and women do view this slightly differently, with men welcoming it as of greater importance and seeing it more positively.

2. Communications have been transformed by the **Information Technology Revolution**. The term "the global village" has been coined to reflect instantaneous and inexpensive telecommunications access by voice, facsimile or multi-media to all corners of the world. All of the information and discoveries of modern science have become widely available as a result of the technology

and communications revolutions. Electronic and desk-top publishing processes have transformed the economics of knowledge transfer. These processes make redundant the idea that partial knowledge and information is power. There are now no secrets that telecommunications cannot break at a competitive price. Technology has made them accessible and is democratising knowledge and information, for those with skills. This means that jobs which depended on using and keeping secret information are no longer secure or relevant. They are increasingly at risk from technologically driven competition. Information and knowledge are now inexpensive, and industries based on the new technologies have made it their business to deliver know-how in world markets at a low cost. It is available directly to companies and individuals alike on the Internet.

3. **The Know-How Revolution** fuelled the growth of knowledge-based businesses made possible by the information technology and communications revolutions. The know-how revolution was, however, just part of a wider explosion of service businesses which constituted a revolution in their own right

4. **The Services Revolution.** It is now accepted that manufacturing jobs have disappeared from the developed Western economies and have been transferred to the lower-cost economies of the rapidly developing Eastern and Southern Hemispheres. The Century of the Pacific refers not only to the industrial might of Japan but also to the phenomenal market growth of the Newly Industrialising Countries (NICs or "tigers") of South East Asia, including Hong Kong, Singapore, Taiwan and Korea. The NICs have started competing with the West in services as well as in manufacturing, and between 70 per cent and 90 per cent of new jobs created in the main developed countries are now in the service sector.

5. **The Marketing or Customer Revolution** has accompanied the revolutions mentioned above. Power has shifted from the producers to the consumers who, helped by deregulation, world wide competition and much greater sophistication of information and choice, are exercising their increasing knowledge and power to

purchase shrewdly. Now it is not so much a question of producers selling what they make, but of finding out their customers' needs and turning them into commercial requirements which can be met profitably. The five revolutions in information technology, communications, know-how, services, and marketing have radically altered the shape of organisations and the patterns of work for employees. The shrinking of the professional core of the organisation has much reduced the number of permanent jobs and increased the use of sub-contractors.

6. As a result, the **Labour Market** has undergone its own radical transformation. A revolutionary shift has occurred from unitary to more diversified and flexible patterns of work and careers, leading to a revolution in career structures. Employer-employee contracts have been redrawn all over the world, with mutual expectations changing. Despite this, there is still a huge risk involved in entering into any sort of working relationship. It is seen as one of the biggest upheavals in one's life.

7. **Career Structures** have been revolutionised correspondingly. Rewards are no longer based on promotion upwards through the rungs of a vertical career ladder. People are now rewarded for short-term performance in meeting current job requirements.

8. The revolution in **Employee Expectations** is a direct result of the structural labour market and career changes, with employees seeking immediate rewards for work done. They also look for employers to invest in the bottom line of their career biography, and to brand their curriculum vitae with the hallmark of blue-chip experience. This is an important ingredient of maintaining employability and marketability in the post-employment market places of the future. (Paradoxically, although corporations have recently been seeking to employ fewer and fewer people they increasingly require their subcontractors to have particular, in-depth kinds of corporate experience.) Feeling valued is often the most important factor in job satisfaction, and should never be ignored, whatever the employment status. Adequate resources, challenges and a suitable environment are also vital but in the ever-changing work place these can be difficult to sustain.

9. The revolution in **Employer Requirements** has involved moving away from "inputs" based on tenure, service, loyalty, qualifications and good behaviour, towards "outputs" based on contribution, performance, productivity and short term results. This shorter term, more performance- and output- orientated approach has knock-on effects,the most significant of which is the tenth revolutionary change below.

10. The revolution in *Pay Performance and Reward* has involved the shift away from the graded pay scales of incremental structures and promotional ladders. The move has been towards basic pay linked to competencies and variable cash rewards as an increasingly significant proportion of total remuneration packages, based upon individual, team and corporate performance.

New Directions

Table 12.1 New Directions in the Post Employment Society

- The flexible firm: contracting out, competitive tendering
- Shamrocks, federations & doughnuts
- The flexible workforce
- Flexible lives and careers
- Investors in people
- Training, development and re-education
- Counselling, coaching and mentoring.

The future world of work predicted by Charles Handy, in which organisations are described in graphic metaphors of shamrocks, federations and doughnuts, has already arrived in different guises and places. So, we are moving in the direction of the flexible firm both with private sector outsourcing and contracting out, and with public sector compulsory competitive tendering.

The flexible workforce is here, partly by default, through involuntary downsizing and early retirements – but partly too because individuals are now increasingly choosing to seize control of their own lives. They wish to lead flexible lives and careers, and are encouraged to invest in life-long learning themselves, alongside government exhortations for companies to become *investors in people* through training, development and re-education. However, this quest for flexible lives and careers intrinsically carries with it a degree of associated frustration, uncertainty and insecurity against a background of tightly controlled pay, higher performance expectations, feelings of being less valued for work carried out and fears of harsh "traditional" staff reductions. Naturally, such conditions may lead to stress and other health problems. We have seen a move away from the management styles of command-and-control to more leadership, and the quest for building supportive cultures based on the values and techniques of counselling, coaching and mentoring. Paradoxically, the flexible workforce needs more attention to staff well-being, including that of subcontractors and associates, rather than less.

The Need for a New Vocabulary in the Post-Employment Society

The future of work therefore calls for a new vocabulary to facilitate communication, mutual understanding and exchange in the new markets of the global economy and cyberspace. This is not just a shift in language but a new way of thinking, acting and relating to the other participants in the labour market. A move from the old Big Idea of security from the outside to the new Big Idea of resourcefulness and security from within.

The New Vocabulary

From labour force to work resource?

- Away from age and position
- Towards skills, potential and life experience
- Thinking laterally about the talent pool
- Accessing new ways of tapping the work resource
- Viewing the employee as customer or consumer

- Accepting individual accountability for own learning
- Encouraging organisational learning
- Enabling an environment for learning
- Creating learning incentives and rewards
- With employees investing for professional development (capital account)
- And employees selling services for salary/fees (revenue account).

The New Vocabulary should help to shift the paradigms in which we think about work away from a concept of belonging to a labour market towards thinking of individuals as a marketable work resource. This implies a move away from valuing age and position *per se*, towards sharing skills, potential and life experience; trading with economic entities that can make creative use of the talent pool and access new ways of tapping the work resource. Such a new vocabulary is one that treats the employee as a customer or consumer of the management style, culture and services of the organisation. The individual accepts accountability for their own learning, while the company encourages organisational learning, enables an environment for learning, and creates learning incentives and rewards. This provides a framework in which employees invest part of their working lives for professional development (on capital account) as well as one in which employees see themselves as selling services for salary/fees (on revenue account).

Above all the unit of account is now the personal marketability of the individual, which has become paramount in personal and career survival. As indicated in Chapter 1, for the past century a significant proportion of the population have had their identities, careers and very lives shaped by the concept of employment work. The changes that have taken place over the span of a normal lifetime are quite staggering. They are even more remarkable when viewed in historical context.

The impact of corporate change on individuals has been to force them to a point where their personal marketability is now the paramount consideration in individual and career survival. This can of course include marketability to other employers for more or less traditional jobs of a quasi-career variety. It certainly includes internal as well as external marketability. But above all, it means the individual taking control of and responsibility for his or her own marketability, planning for it, investing in it, managing it and developing it for the future.

John Thompson of Brunel University at the IPD Third Age Forum Conference referred to in Chapter 2, argued that employability depends upon individuals developing a portfolio of transferable skills. He identified five core training and skill fields, as follows:

1. Career management
2. Coaching and mentoring
3. Change management
4. Networking and contracting
5. Internal (and external) consultancy.

The Forum argued that portfolio workers of any age, and particularly those in the Third Age, should develop their range and repertoire in these core skills in order to survive and thrive in the post-employment society. The new vocabulary is needed to enable new ways of thinking, earning, learning and living in the post-employment society.

The *Independent on Sunday* Review for 23 June 1996 was devoted to the topic of such new ways of "Downshifting, voluntary simplicity and other ways out of the rat race", and described new patterns of life that are emerging after the main career. In particular, it noted that increasingly people are not waiting passively for a Third Age experience to be thrust upon them abruptly around age fifty through involuntary redundancy or early retirement; rather, they are taking action into their own hands earlier and "opting out" for lower incomes and simpler lives of their own accord.

Though such moves have become known as "downshifting", it could conversely be seen as "upshifting". If quality of life is a priority, then the independence achieved through pursuing a chosen portfolio of work should surely be regarded as an upwards rather than a downwards movement! Most of us have internalised the view that corporate life (commercial or professional) is the preferred existence and the principal means and measure of career progression. This is where, with Charles Handy and many others, we believe that a radical approach is necessary to challenge the traditional paradigms.

The Independent Review article explains the philosophy of Handy, who remains the pre-eminent authority and role model for the port-folio life and "The chance to live more than once"... The way in which Charles and his wife Elizabeth organise their lives, how they balance their separate requirements, interests and workloads, and how they enjoy life to the full without being overburdened, demonstrates the pragmatic theme of this book in no small measure.

The age at which people seek alternative careers and lives is reducing markedly. People in their mid thirties with fifteen or twenty years service are now leaving companies at or just before the end of their "useful life" with that firm. Such movement creates choices and opportunities undreamed of by earlier generations. For some dual-career couples wishing to look after or extend a young family, a lump sum severance payment from one partner's former employer may come at a convenient time and keep one parent at home, looking after the family and saving on domestic help while the other is at work. Equally, a measure of role reversal can leave one partner of either gender looking after the babies and starting a self-employed business from home, so that the other earns money to pay the short term bills while a medium-term shift in living arrangements is created. Twenty or thirty years ago such a way of life would have been virtually unthinkable. So a completely new and much more flexible approach to work is opening up.

Having the courage to break the mould depends, we suggest, on staying closely in touch with one's inner feelings, on taking a consid-ered personal view of life priorities and aspirations, on careful life planning; and on acting, now, in a way that makes sense for you, your partner and your dependants. Which stage are you, the reader, now at? Whatever your age or phase of life, the chance to live more than once should be seized with vigour – you will never regret it.

Appendix 1
The Story of Future Perfect

A small working group of people with notable business, personnel or academic backgrounds started to meet in 1987. The group had been brought together by John Ottensooser, a senior financial adviser with Allied Dunbar, who had a vision about the potential of the Third Age for each one of us, in contrast to the negative connotations of retirement. He wanted to explore how this vision could be translated into providing practical .support for individuals approaching their Third Age, to stimulate and encourage the positive aspects of transition. The group included Professor Charles Handy of the London Business School, Parry Rogers, Chairman of BTEC and formerly Personnel Director of IBM and Plessey, Dennis Stevenson, Chairman of SRU, Director of Pearson and Chairman of the Trustees of the Tate Gallery, and Barry Curnow, then Chairman and Chief Executive of MSL International.

The group soon came to appreciate the powerful implications of the issues they were considering; the social and economic trends involved pointed to the emergence of a potentially critical situation for the UK in the future, affecting both companies and individuals in significant ways. These perceptions were well in advance of public awareness or recognition by corporations of the changes that would materialise progressively over the next decade.

The group believed that provision of relevant Third Age transition support could form the basis of a new business. Such a business would not only be able to make a valuable contribution to the UK managerial and professional population (the initial target), but should also be able to provide a financial return on the funds required to mount the activities involved. Consequently a suitable business plan was drawn up with the help of Arthur Anderson and Co., funds pledged by group members as share capital, and a potential chief executive sought to launch the new company. It was decided to call the company 'Future Perfect', following an inspiration by John's wife, Sheila.

Various preparatory moves to create the new business were made during 1988, and John McLean Fox, a Director of the PA Consulting Group, was appointed Chief Executive, to commence on 1 April 1989. The new company came into operation at that time, with a staff of two, John Lumbard and Jean Marzetti. The official launch of the company came a little while later, on 24 May 1989, and took the form of a reception at the City of London Club with some 100 guests. The gathering was addressed by Parry Rogers, Future Perfect's first Chairman, by John McLean Fox, its Chief Executive, followed by a launch endorsement from the Right Honourable Michael Heseltine, MP, who felt that an appropriate message to Third Agers was 'Past tense, Future Perfect'. The company thus started off with widespread support for the underlying concept and the objectives outlined.

The Board, which consisted mainly of the original working group, decided that the company's target market should consist initially of managerial and professional staff in large corporations, and that the service offerings of Future Perfect should address this specific population. The company therefore started to carry out appropriate research and develop suitable products for this market, the content of which forms much of the material to be found in this book. The first Future Perfect workshop for individuals and couples was held in September 1989, based on development work carried out by John McLean Fox with the help of Jinny Ditzler and Gary Davies, specialist coaches in the personal development field, and Derek Hill, now head of Counselling at Relate. The methodology launched and developed through these initial workshops provided the foundation for Future Perfect's subsequent workshop and counselling activities, carried out principally with the help of associates Greta Colman, John Downs, Maggie Hammond, and Brian Morton. Barry Curnow, a founder director, became Chairman in 1991, and Future Perfect continues to make progress in assisting both companies and individuals to deal with significant career transition issues. The company is about to enter a new phase of development on this front in order to capitalise on the substantial experience already gained in this specialist field.

Appendix 2
Age And Employment
(An IPD Publication)

BACKGROUND

Age discrimination in employment can:

- affect anybody regardless of how old they are
- reduce employment prospects for older people, younger people and women returners
- favour people in the age group twenty-five to thirty-five
- prevent the full consideration of abilities, potential and experience.

AIMS

This summary:

- argues the case for employment practices which do not discriminate on the grounds of age
- presents the case for a voluntary approach rather than statutory regulation
- sets out an action plan and recommendations for avoiding the use of age and age-related criteria in employment.

VIEWPOINT

The Institute of Personnel and Development is committed to the removal of age discrimination in employment because it is wasteful of talent and harmful to both individuals and organisations. The use of age, age bands and age-related criteria reduces objectivity in employment decision-making and increases the likelihood of inappropriate decisions.

Employment decisions based on age are never justifiable because:

- age is not a genuine employment criterion
- age is a poor predicator of performance
- it is misleading to equate physical and mental ability with age.

The efficient and effective use of people's skills requires that employment decisions should be based on competencies; qualifications; skills; potential and objective, job-related criteria obtained through careful analysis of job requirements and job performance.

The IPD believes there is an important business case for employers to take action to remove age discrimination and has undertaken research and published guidance to raise awareness and educate personnel practitioners and employers about the issues involved.

Although the IPD recognises that the law can help to effect change in employment practice, self-regulation based on increased understanding is favoured as the best way to encourage employers to deal with age discrimination.

AN ACTION PLAN

Review

- Scrutinise all personnel policies, practices and procedures because age discrimination can:
  - occur anywhere in the employment cycle from recruitment to redundancy
  - be blatant or subtle, direct or indirect.

Policy

- Implement policy as part of an approach to equal opportunities.
- Use only objective job-related criteria essential for satisfactory performance.
- Communicate policy to all managers and employees.

Stance and key actions

- Do not use age, age guidelines and age-related criteria.
- Challenge the use of age and age-related criteria in every aspect of employment decision-making.
- Educate and train all staff about the implications of age discrimination.
- Only use dates of birth for monitoring purposes and administration. Give written assurances on this to gain the confidence of people and commitment of staff making employment decisions.
- Monitor the age profile of the organisation at regular intervals to identify evidence of unfair discrimination against particular age groups.
- Consider ways of making sure that all age groups have access to development and promotion opportunities.

AGE DISCRIMINATION COSTS

Organisation which fail to tackle age discrimination will be at a disadvantage in the recruitment and retention of talented employees.

Organisations need to develop the talents of all their employees to be successful in an increasingly competitive market place.

AGE DISCRIMINATION AND THE LAW

There is no law against age discrimination in employment in the United Kingdom, however:

- indirect sex discrimination can be claimed under the Sex Discrimination Act of 1975
- the claim can be made if statistical evidence shows that age criteria makes it more difficult for one sex to compete equally against the other.

Available evidence does not make a strong case for legal action to remove age discrimination:

- in France the introduction of legislation made little change in the full-time employment rates of older workers
- French legislation made older workers less attractive to employers.

Employment Department Research in 1994 found that:

- the USA, Canada, France, Australia, New Zealand and Spain had enacted age-related legislation but that it was hard to identify the effects on the labour markets
- even though there has been legislation in the United States for over 25 years, statutory protection remains incomplete and ineffective.

The UK Government set up the Advisory Group on Older Workers in February 1993 to address the issue through the 'Getting On' national campaign. This promotes action by employers, recruitment agencies and others, to drop the use of age and age-related criteria in decision-making. It also produces publications to raise awareness and increase understanding.

There is growing evidence of UK employers taking voluntary action to regulate their own working practices.

Organisations in the public, private and voluntary sectors have developed ways of raising awareness, including the IPD, the Department of Employment, the Carnegie Third Age Programme, Age Concern, METRA Services Ltd and the Local Government Management Board.

These organisations have worked hard to encourage the development of employment practices which address age discrimination.

RECOMMENDATIONS

Each stage of the employment cycle should be examined as follows:

Recruitment and selection

- *Advertising*
  Age, age-related criteria or age ranges should not be used in advertisements other than to encourage applications from age groups which do not usually apply. Where this is the case the purpose should be made clear.

- *Application forms*
  It is desirable to state that age criteria will not be taken into account in employment decisions but only for monitoring purposes and for this to be asked for in a 'tear-off' section of the application form.

- *Interviews*
  Interviewers and those concerned with selection must be aware that prejudices

and stereotypical views about age are dangerous, as is judging and individual's age on the basis of physical characteristics.

Medical advice

An individual's age should not be used in order to make judgements about their abilities or fitness. Where such a judgement is required and occupational health or medical practitioner should be consulted.

Reward

Pay and terms of employment should not be based on age-related criteria, but should reflect individual standards of job performance and the value of their contribution to overall objectives.

Training and development

It is inefficient to automatically exclude particular age groups from training and development programmes.

Retention and redundancy

When releasing employees, the future needs for knowledge, skills and competencies should be taken into account.

Alternatives to redundancy should be considered such as shorter hours, part-time working, contractual arrangements, secondments – perhaps employment breaks.

Retirement

Research indicates that many older workers would welcome an opportunity:

- for phased retirement
- for flexible working
- to work beyond the normal retirement age
- to work on a self-employed basis
- to work in the voluntary sector.

Organisations should also consider the advantages of using retirees as mentors to pass on experience and help to other employees.

KEY POINTS

- By the year 2000 it is estimated that one person in three in employment will be over 40.
- Demographic changes are altering the age profile of the labour market which will soon contain more people aged over 40 than younger people.
- Evidence shows that differences in absenteeism between age groups are marginal.
- Pension funds are having to adjust the ageing of the population.
- Many employers are already taking action on age discrimination as a way of keeping ahead of their competitors.
- More people are living longer, active and healthier lives.

- Older workers stay in their jobs longer than younger people.
- Age discrimination leads to under-achievement, reduced self-confidence and motivation, lower self-esteem and loss of personal income or status.
- Over-targeting of favoured age groups can lead to inflated labour costs.
- Findings from many studies show that both younger and older workers are on their average equally effective in their work.
- Public support is growing for the introduction of a law to prevent age discrimination.
- Research shows that given the right training older people are just as capable of learning new skills as younger people.
- Many older workers would welcome phased retirement and part-time or flexible working.

QUOTES

B&Q

"B&Q welcomes older job applicants. It has a positive policy on recruiting older workers and retaining those who are nearing retirement age and this has provided the company with a stock of experienced and customer friendly staff. The recruitment strategy proved to B&Q managers, the public and older people alike, that a policy of hiring older people can work and that older employees can make a significant and valuable contribution to the success of a company."

WH Smith Group

"WH Smith has a recruitment policy which sets out to ensure the best person for the job. In order to improve the retention rate of staff, those responsible for recruitment and selection are required to ensure that age is not used as a criterion. We have found that turnover rates for older workers are significantly lower. Every one per cent of staff turnover costs our business £800,000, so reducing staff turnover represents a huge opportunity for cost savings."

Sainsbury's

"Customer service is a high priority for us at Sainsbury's, and it is helpful to us if our staff reflect the customer base we serve. For example, older workers can easily identify with the large number of retired people who shop in our stores. Their experience and natural courtesy are particularly helpful in enabling us to meet our high standards of customer care."

The Littlewoods Organisation plc

"The recruitment policy of the Littlewoods Organisation plc maximises the potential of all employees, regardless of age. It ensures that we recruit the best person for the job because it makes good business sense."

USEFUL ADDRESSES

Advisory Group on Older Workers
Department for Education and Employment
Sanctuary Buildings
Great Smith St
London SW1P 3BT
Tel: 0171 925 5000
Fax: 0171 925 6186

The Carnegie Third Age Programme
3 Robert St
London WC2N 6BN
Tel: 0171 976 1785
Fax: 0171 839 3019

The Third Age Challenge Trust
Anglia House
115 Commercial Road
Swindon SW1 5PL
Tel: 01793 533370
Fax: 01793 533390

Employers Forum on Age
Astral House
1268 London Road
London SW16 4ER
Tel: 0181 679 1075
Fax: 0181 679 6069

The Federation of Recruitment and Employment Services
36-38 Mortimer St
London W1N 7RB
Tel: 0171 323 4300
Fax: 0171 255 2878

Local Government Management Board
38 Belgrave Square
London SW1X 8NZ
Tel: 0171 235 6081
Fax: 0171 235 1257

METRA Services Ltd
PO Box 1540
Homer Road
Solihull
West Midlands B91 3QB
Tel: 0121 704 6699
Fax: 0121 711 1294

READING LIST

Carnegie United Kingdom Trust, *The Carnegie Inquiry Into the Third Age: Final Report: Life, Work and Livelihood in the Third Age*, Dunfermline, 1993.

Department for Education and Employment, *Age Works*, London, 1995.

Department for Education and Employment, *Getting On: The Benefits of an Older WOrkforce*, London, 1995.

Department for Education and Employment, *Too Old...Who Says? Advice for Older Workers*, London, 1995.

Institute of Personnel Management, *Age and Employment: Policies, Attitudes and Practice*, London, 1993.

Itzin, Catherine and Phillipson, Chris, *Age Barriers at Work: Maximising the Potential of Mature and Older People*, Metropolitan Authorities Recruitment Agency, Solihull, 1993.

METRA Services and Local Government Management Board, *Employment of Older Workers and Age Auditing: Policy and Practice in Local Government*, London, 1995.

Metropolitan Authorities Recruitment Agency, *Lifting the Age Barrier: A Practical Guide*, Solihull, 1994.

Moore, Joanne, Tilson, Barbara, and Whitting, Gill, *An International Overview of Employment Policies and Practices towards Older Workers*, Metropolitan Authorities Recruitment Agency, Solihull, 1994.

Naylor, Peter, *Age No Barrier: Developing Policies for the Employment and Re-employment of the Older Worker,* Metropolitan Authorities Recruitment Agency, Solihull, 1990.

Worsley, Richard, *Age and Employment: Why Workers Should Think Again About Older Workers*, Age Concern, London, 1996.

This extract is taken from Key Facts on Age and Employment by the Institute of Personnel and Development and reproduced with permission of the publishers, The Institute of Personnel and Development, IPD House, 35 Camp Road, London SW19 4YX.

Appendix 3
Survey Questionnaire

We set out below the text of the questionnaire used in the Survey of Third Agers conducted for this book:

BASIC INFORMATION

Name: *Age:*

Main career role(s):

When was the transition made from your main role?

Which are now your main roles, and approximately what proportion of your time do you allocate to each one?

                                                    Percentage of time

First:

Second:

Third:

Fourth:

Fifth:

Sixth:

Any other:

TRANSITION IMPLICATIONS

What were the particular challenges for you in making the transition?

Did your firm help you?   *If so, in what ways?*

In retrospect, what else could they have done?

What do you most enjoy about your current portfolio of activities?

What do you most miss from your previous existence?

What would you like to change still further?

Has money been a significant issue? If so, in what way?

Given the opportunity, would you have welcomed making a change earlier?

Do you have any regrets about being in your current situation? If so, what?

How has your partner (if applicable) been affected by tour transition?

SOME DEEPER REFLECTIONS

What has impresses or surprised you about this new phase in life following your main career?

How do you view the future? What hope, fears, aims and objectives do you have?

How do you feel now about health, wealth, work and happiness?

Please would you write a succinct paragraph on the advice you would give to a younger colleague approaching transition from their main career (at any age from 40 plus)?

THIRD AGE WORK FIELDS

We are planning to write at some length about each of the main fields of activity engaged in by Third Agers. It would be helpful if you could write a few sentences related to your chosen field(s) in response to the question 'How is it working out?'

Operating independently as a self-employed contractor:

Becoming a specialist consultant:

Fulfilling the role of a Non-Executive Director:

Starting up a new manufacturing or service business venture with others:

Working for the Community or for a Charity:

Other forms of 'Gift Work'

The authors/researchers may be contacted at:

> *10 Maresfield Gardens*
> *London NW3 5SU*
> *Telephone: 0171 435 9316*
> *Fax: 0171 431 6084*

Appendix 4
The Changing Dimensions of Post-Employment Work Markets

This appendix summarises some of the more important dimensions of change in the new employment markets and environment described in this book.

Table A4.1 Dimensions of Change in the Future of Work

- European Third Agers :1990 31%; to 42% in 2020
- Pensioners 30% Working Agers to 42% in 2030
- U.S. Knowledge Workers 17% in 1950 to 60% 1990
- 24m Employees in 1988 (16.3m full-time)
- 24m in 2000 (12m full-time)
- Active men 55-64, down 23% U.K,33% Netherlands,1970-88
- 40% school leavers without a GCSE, 18% to H.E.
- 4m. telecommuters 1995 to 35% working population by 2000
- Managers changed company once in 1939, 7 x now.

The number of European third agers will rise from a figure of 31 per cent in 1990 to 42 per cent in 2020, while the corresponding figure for pensioners will increase from 30 per cent of the working agers to 42 per cent in 2030. Behind this shift is a picture of increasing consumer power and political influence for the third ager in society but, at the same time, rising costs of employing the older workers who do remain in companies.

The number of knowledge workers in the USA rose from 17 per cent in 1950 to 60 per cent 1990, a remarkable shift towards the information society.

The total number of UK employees is predicted to remain static at 24m, the same figure as in 1988. However a huge shift is taking place in the structure of employment. In 1988, 16m of those employees were full-time whereas in 2000 only 12m of them will be.

Activity rates for men aged 55-64, which is the figure for actual participation in the workforce by those available to do so, fell by 23 per cent in the U.K, and by 33 per cent in the Netherlands, during the period 1970-88.

In Britain, 40 per cent of school leavers leave the full-time education system without a GCSE, while only 18 per cent go on to Higher Education.

There were estimated to be some 4 million telecommuters in 1995 (17 per cent of the working population), a figure which is forecast to rise to 35 per cent, i.e. 8 million, by the year 2000. In 1939 managers changed company once on average during their careers, whereas the figure is now seven times.

The most widespread change is the development within the information technology field. However, staff cutbacks, top management changes, cost reduction programmes and reduction in management layers also occur and are unlikely to take place in isolation. The pace of change is unpredictable but always apparent.

The Demographic Time Bomb, Part II

"The wrinklies rule ok!?"

Everybody has heard of the Demographic Time Bomb, Part l, which referred to the disappearing battalions of young people caused by reduced fertility rates in the developed world. However the implications of its corollary, the Demographic Time Bomb, Part II, which has also been called the Grey Revolution or Silver Power, have been less well celebrated or understood until recently, particularly by employers. The recent launch in the UK of **The Employers Forum on Age** under the auspices of Howard Davies, Deputy Governor of the Bank of England, shows some sign that awareness is gradually dawning of the revolutionary dimensions of this shift; which, in fact, is far more consequential for the developed economies than the disappearing young people.

Organisations now have to adjust their sights because in the year 2020, Charles Handy predicts, half the number of employees will be paid twice as much for doing three times the work.

During the course of this century, we shall have moved from the 47 x 47x 47 formula, where the typical male worked for 47 hours a week for 47 weeks a year for 47 years of their lives, to a 30 x 30 x 30 formula: people working 30 hours a week for 30 weeks a year for 30 years. Social legislation in Europe is reinforcing this current trend. However, if we apply Handy's principle, this could convert by the year 2020 to something like 70 x 48 x15, or 70 hours a week for 48 weeks a year for an average main career span of just 15 years. This indicates movement into the Third Age at just 36-40 years of age!

So, we face a decrease in young people, particularly the educated and skilled – although there are at the same time growing proportions of the reducing populations of young people going to an increasing number of universities of widely varying calibre. This leads to an experience gap in flatter organisational structures alongside dramatic increases in the numbers of older people; more women returners; more part-time, variable, non-traditional work; career breaks for all, and a changing balance of power in society, the workforce and companies, families and communities.

The Changing Balance of Power in the Post-Employment Society

Table A4.2 Changing Balance of Power

- Old to young in companies
- Young to old in young force
- Leaders to led
- Supplier to customer
- Internal to external relationships
- Controlling to caring, supportive employer
- Internal costs to external investment.

The balance of power is changing from old to young in companies and from young to old in the labour force. At the same time the leaders are increasingly losing power to the led, which is a repeated pattern in the shift from supplier to customer and from internal to external relationships. Labour market power is shifting from the controlling to the caring, supportive employers, particularly those who offer a new deal to their knowledge workers. This may include an investment in their future employability, which is itself an example of a further power shift from internal costs to external investment

Managers are working the longest hours of all groups at the moment which causes some resentment even though it is seen as largely necessary. However, interestingly enough, they seem to spend the least time in front of a computer screen of all the groups of workers employed. Obviously, this can lead to a skills gap if not managed correctly.

Professional and private lives need to be balanced otherwise stress and health problems are likely to emerge. With these difficulties will come insecurities and loss in levels of satisfaction.

The changing balances of power need to be closely monitored because in the short term they may be seen as largely negative. Viewed in isolation, staff cutbacks, changes in top management, cost reduction, few and/or more management layers, outsourcing, relocation, take-overs and mergers will cause unrest and discontent. Hence the need for efficient communication systems and information technology.

Recommended Reading

Open University, The, *Planning Retirement*, Choice Publications, 1982.

Allen, J. and Pifer, A., *Women on the Front Lines*, Urban Institute Press, 1993.

Bolles, R.N., *What Color is Your Parachute?*, Ten Speed Press, annually.

Brown, R., *Good Retirement Guide*, Kogan Page, annually.

Carnegie UK Trust, *Carnegie Inquiry into the Third Age*, 1993.

Coulson-Thomas, C., *Too Old at 40?*, Institute of Management, 1989.

Dewar, F., *Live for a Change*, Darton, Longman & Todd, 1988.

Directorate-General for Employment, Industrial Relations and Social Affairs, *Social Europe, 1993: European Year of Older People and Solidarity Between Generations*, Commission of the European Communities, 1993.

European Community Observatory, *Social and Economic Policies and Older People*, Commission of the European Communities, 1993.

Erikson, E. H., *Childhood and Society*, Paladin, 1977.

Golzen, G., *Going Freelance*, Kogan Page, 1989.

Green, C., 'Making the Most of Older People at Work', an MA dissertation, 1992.

Handy, C., *The Age of Unreason*, Hutchinson, 1989.

Handy, C., *The Empty Raincoat*, Hutchinson, 1994.

Hornby, M., *I Can Do That*, Delta Management, 1993.

Hopson, B. and Scally, M., *Build Your Own Rainbow: A Workbook for Career and Life Management*, Management Books 2000, 1991.

ICAS, *EAPs and Counselling Provision in UK Organisations 1993: An ICAS Report and Policy Guide*, 1993.

Jong, E., *Fear of Fifty*, Chatto & Windus, 1994.

Laslett, P., *A Fresh Map of Life: The Emergence of the Third Age*, Weidenfeld, 1989.

Levinson, D. J., *The Seasons of a Man's Life*, Ballantine Books, 1978.

Macnab, F., *The 30 Vital Years*, John Wiley & Sons, 1992.

Maloney, T. W., and Paul, B., 'Enabling Older Americans to Work' in *1989 Annual Report of the Commonwealth Fund*, 1989.

De Mello, A., *Awareness*, Harper Collins, 1990.

OECD, *Employment Outlook: July 1992*, 1992.

OECD, *Ageing Populations: The Social Policy Implications*, 1992.

Redfield, J., *The Celestine Prophecy*, Bantam Books, 1994.

Schuller, T. and Walker, A., *The Time of Our Life: Education, Employment and Retirement in the Third Age*, Institute for Public Policy Research, 1990.

Sheehy, G., *Passages*, Bantam Books, 1976.

Sheehy, G., *Pathfinders*, Bantam Books, 1982.

Smith, M., *Changing Course*, Management Books 2000, 1992.

Worsley, R., *Age and Employment*, ACE Books, 1996.

Index